THE SHIA-SUNNI DEBATE: ANSWERING THE 50 MOST COMMON QUESTIONS

THE SHIA-SUNNI DEBATE: ANSWERING THE 50 MOST COMMON QUESTIONS

This book is dedicated to
The Ahlul Bayt and The 12th Living Imam
Muhammad Mahdi (AS)

Compiled by Dr Liaket Dewji & Baqerali Alidina
Published by Hyderi Islamic Centre
in association with Sun Behind The Cloud Publications Ltd
Copyright © Hyderi Islamic Centre 2012

ISBN: 978-1-908110-02-2

Printed and bound in the UK by Minuteman Press

Hyderi Islamic Centre
26 Estreham Road, London SW16 5PQ
Email : hyderi@hyderi.org.uk
Telephone : +44 (0)208 769 7553

www.hyderi.org

In the name of Allah (SWT),
The Benficient, The Most Merciful

"Praise is due to Allah (SWT) whose worth cannot be described by speakers, whose bounties cannot be counted by counters and whose claim (to obedience) cannot be satisfied by those who attempt to do so, whom the height of intellectual courage cannot appreciate, and the height of human understanding cannot reach; He for whose description no limit has been laid down, no eulogy exists, no time is ordained and no duration is fixed. He brought forth creation through His Omnipotence, dispersed winds through His Compassion, and made firm the shaking earth with mountains and rocks."

Imam Ali Ibn Abu Talib (AS)
First Sermon: Nahjul Balagha

CONTENTS

Chapter 2: The Ahlul Bayt
(The Prophet's Household) 45

Chapter 3: The Companions and
Miscellaneous issues 69

PREFACE

Hyderi Islamic Centre, was honoured and privileged to have a world-renowned speaker address the community for five days in January 2012 (Islamic year: Safar 1433). This was to commemorate the tragedy of Kerbala, when Imam Husayn (AS) the grandson of the Holy Prophet (SAW), was martyred in Kerbala, in Iraq more than 1,400 years ago.

The topic covered during these five days was based on answering: "The 50 most common questions posed by Ahle Sunnah to Shia Muslims".

At the request of Hyderi members, this book and publication has been compiled, and attempts to resolve major theological differences, in the form of Questions and Answers so that the knowledge can be shared with other readers.

Our thanks to Shaykh Mohammed Abbas Panju, who has recently graduated from his studies in Najaf and become the resident aalim at Hyderi Islamic Centre. His encouragement and scholarly review have proved invaluable and to Tehseen Merali from Sun Behind The Cloud Publications for her advice and help in publishing the work. Lastly, we would also like to thank Reshma Jaffrey and Sameer Abedi for their contribution to this book. Your rewards are with the Almighty.

We hope and pray that the answers and comments in response to these 50 common questions will help bridge the gap of understanding between Shias and Sunni Muslims. For this reason, all of the answers are provided with references from the Holy Qur'an and books compiled and written by leading Ahle Sunnah Scholars.

All the knowledge contained in this book is by the Grace of Allah (SWT) and any mistakes or errors are through our weaknesses, fallibility or misunderstanding. We ask Allah (SWT) to forgive us if we have offended any reader, Muslim or non-Muslim, Sunni or Shia.

Dr Liaket Dewji and Baqerali Alidina

12th May 2012 / 20th Jamadil-al-thani 1433
Wiladat of Lady Fatima (AS)

INTRODUCTION

One of the greatest tragedies for the Islamic ummah, the global Muslim community, is that at a time when we should be united, we have never been more divided. The religious divide, in particular, is increasing with wars, conflicts and disputes engulfing the different sects of Islam in various Muslim and non-Muslim countries.

The truth is that all Muslims believe in:
- One God (Allah SWT)
- One Book (The Holy Qur'an)
- One Kabah (in Makkah)
- The final Prophet – Muhammad (SAW)

This common ground should be used as the base to build theological unity and prevent further divisions between Muslims – divisions which have lead to the killing and maiming of fellow human beings in the name of Islam.

Shia Muslims, who form only 15% of the worldwide Muslim population, have been persecuted and oppressed for the past 14 centuries. The main reason for this is because Shia Muslims have been misunderstood, and misrepresented, in the way they follow Islamic tradition as prescribed by the Holy Qur'an and the ahadith (sayings/ practises) of the Holy Prophet (SAW), and the Ahlul Bayt (Household of the Prophet).

This book has been compiled in five chapters, covering the lectures delivered at Hyderi Islamic Centre in January 2012. It attempts to answer the 50 most common questions posed by Ahle Sunnah to Shia Muslims. The response and comments to each of these 50 questions are provided and based on:

- The Holy Qur'an

- The traditions (Hadith) of the Holy Prophet (SAW) documented in reference books compiled by leading Ahle Sunnah Scholars (and not from Shia books).

- Common sense and reason – "aql".

In his last sermon, delivered at Ghadeer Khumm between Makkah and Madinah, the Holy Prophet (SAW) said:

- "I am leaving among you two weighty things: the one being the Book of Allah in which there is right guidance and light, so hold fast to the Book of Allah and adhere to it.. . .

- The second are the members of my household, I remind you (of your duties) to the members of my family."

[Narrated in Sahi Muslim, Book No.31, Tradition (Hadith) No.5920]

Allah (SWT) has blessed us with the power of reasoning. This gift should be utilised to read and ponder over the fifty Q&A provided and to share the knowledge with others.

We trust that this publication, will lead to a better understanding of true Islam by both Muslims and non-Muslims, Sunnis and Shias.

Abbreviations and Glossary of Terms

Ahlul Bayt	The Prophet's (SAW) Household
Alam	Standard, flag – symbol of Ahlul Bayt.
Allah (SWT)	Arabic word for the one true God
AS	Acronyms that denote honour and respect to the family of the Prophet.
Bay'at	Allegiance
Bid'at	Innovation
Bint	Daughter of...used to provide full name.
Haraam	Prohibitted
Hadith	Tradition narrated or followed by Muslims
Ibn	Son of...used to provide full name
Imam	Leader appointed by Allah (SWT)
Jibraeel	the archangel Gabriel - the angel sent by Allah (SWT) to reveal the Holy Qur'an to the Prophet.
SAW	"Sall allaahu alay-hi wa aalihi wa-sallam" or "May Allah honour him and his family and grant him peace"
Shaitan	Satan/Devil
Shirk	Prohibited beliefs that associate others with God
Ulema	Scholars
Wajib	Compulsory or mandatory

CHAPTER 1
IMAM ALI IBN ABU TALIB (AS)

Question 1: Do Shias worship Ali ibn Abu Talib (AS)?

Shias do not worship Imam Ali (AS). Shias worship Allah (SWT). How can anyone believe that Shias worship Imam Ali (AS) when he himself tells us to worship Allah (SWT)?

1.1 Nahjul Balagha

In the famous book, Nahjul Balagha, a compilation of the sermons and sayings of Imam Ali (AS), the first recorded sermon begins with:

"Praise is due to Allah whose worth cannot be described by speakers, whose bounties cannot be counted by calculators and whose claim (to obedience) cannot be satisfied by those who attempt to do so, whom the height of intellectual courage cannot appreciate, and the divings of understanding cannot reach; He for whose description no limit has been laid down, no eulogy exists, no time is ordained and no duration is fixed. He brought forth creation through His Omnipotence, dispersed winds through His Compassion, and made firm the shaking earth with rocks."

Imam Ali (AS) continues: "The foremost in religion is the acknowledgement of Him, the perfection of acknowledging

Him is to testify Him, the perfection of testifying Him is to believe in His Oneness, the perfection of believing in His Oneness is to regard Him Pure, and the perfection of His purity is to deny Him attributes, because every attribute is a proof that it is different from that to which it is attributed and everything to which something is attributed is different from the attribute. Thus whoever attaches attributes to Allah recognises His like, and who recognises His like regards Him two; and who regards Him two recognises parts for Him; and who recognises parts for Him mistook Him; and he who mistook Him, pointed at Him; and he who pointed at Him, admitted limitations for Him; and he who admitted limitations for Him, numbered Him."

This sermon, and others in Nahjul Balagha show that Imam Ali (AS) is the most eloquent exponent of Allah's existence, His unity (Tawhid).

1.2 Other followers

There are other groups, chief among them the Nuzayris, the various groups of the Ghuluww, the extremists, who have worshipped Ali, but not the Shias.

Shias take pride that Ali (AS) was not Allah but was the first male to worship Allah, with the Prophet (SAW) ; the first to bow down behind Muhammad (SAW), in prayer (salah), in worship of the one true Lord, Allah (SWT).

The Ghuluww, the Nuzayris and others, who take delight in their worship of Ali (AS), are not friends or allies, of the Shias. They are people who have abandoned Islam, who have traduced Ali (AS) by ascribing divinity to him. Too many Shias over the years have praised the Nuzayris and the Ali worshippers in their hymns (marthiyas) and in their religious poetry. This is wrong, un-Islamic and this is something the Prophet (SAW) warned against.

In a famous tradition (hadith) of the Prophet (SAW), narrated by Ahle Sunnah and Shia scholars alike, the Holy Prophet said: "O Ali, you have a resemblance to Prophet Jesus (Isa), the son of Virgin Mary whom some Jews hated so much that they slandered him and his mother Mary and whom some Christians loved so much that they placed him in a position not rightly his."

Shias love Ali (AS) but do not, and should not, put him in a position which is not rightly his, that is, above the Prophet (SAW) or in place of Allah (SWT)

As Imam Ali (AS) himself said, "Two kinds of people will be damned on my account. Those who form an exaggerated opinion about me and those who underestimate me because they hate me." (Nahjul Balaghah, list of short sayings no.116).

So the historical evidence, the consensus of the Shia ulema and common sense are all proofs that that Shias worship Allah (SWT), not Imam Ali (AS).

Question 2: Do Shias believe that Ali ibn Abu Talib (AS) is superior to the Prophet (SAW)?

Some enemies of the Shias claim that, we believe, Imam Ali (AS) was better or superior to Muhammad (SAW); some have suggested that we believe that the revelation of the Holy Qur'an was intended for him but mistakenly given to his cousin Muhammad (SAW). This is nonsense.

2.1 Common sense

Ali ibn Abu Talib (AS) was either 10 or 12 years of age when the Prophet (SAW) received his first revelation, (wahi), from the archangel Jibraeel (Gabriel) in a cave. Does it make sense to believe that Shias would claim Jibraeel, an infallible angel, mistook a 12-year-old boy for a 40-year-old man?

Shias do not believe this but rather take pleasure in pointing out how Imam Ali (AS) slept in the bed of the Prophet (SAW) to protect the Prophet's life. Ali (AS) slept in the Prophet's bed on the night of Hijra so that the Prophet (SAW) could migrate to Madinah safely. How could we then believe he is superior to the Prophet (SAW)?

2.2 References from books of Ahle Sunnah

In fact, the Prophet (SAW) famously predicted, in a tradition (hadith) narrated by very famous Ahle Sunnah scholars like Imam Ahmed ibn Hanbal in his Musnad and Imam Hakim in his Mustadrak: "In truth there will be, among you, one who shall fight over the ta'wil of the Qur'an, the interpretation of the Qur'an, just as I fought over its tanzil, its revelation." Abu Bakr and Umar asked: "Am I he?" The Prophet said: "No, it is the one who is mending the shoes."

The companions turned to the side to see Imam Ali (AS) mending the Prophet's shoes.

This hadith shows that:

- Imam Ali (AS) was the one the Prophet (SAW) singled out to his companions as the protector of Qura'nic interpretation;

- Imam Ali ibn Abu Talib (AS) used to mend the Prophet's shoes and take pride in it.

After the Prophet (SAW), Ali (AS) is the most superior and the greatest being created by Allah (SWT) – but the key point to note here is "after" the Prophet.

Question 3: Where is the proof that Ali (AS) was appointed by the Prophet (SAW)?

This is one of the most important questions to ponder and needs a detailed review. The Shias point to the hadith of Ghadeer Khumm, narrated by the Ahle Sunnah (see below) in which the Holy Prophet (SAW) declared: "Man kunto mawla hu fa haadha Aliyyun mawla" – "Of whomsoever I am mawla, Ali is also his mawla, i.e. leader."

3.1 Does "mawla" mean friend?

This comes up again and again – especially that "mawla" means friend, not leader, imam or amir. We can analyse this by the following:

3.1.1 Meaning of "mawla" ?

According to one study, the word mawla has between 20 and 30 different definitions in Arabic, but only one of which translates as "friend". Most translate it as "owner", "leader", "benefactor", "guide", "helper". Look at the Holy Qur'an, the words, mawla, awla, wali, wilayat, all come from the same root word, "wali", and are all used in the Holy Qur'an to refer to guidance and leadership. For friendship or companionship, the Holy Qur'an tends to use the words, khaleel, sadiq and hameem.

3.1.2 Context when word "mawla" was used

The word "mawla" was used at Ghadeer Khumm, on the return journey from the last pilgrimage (Hajj) of the Prophet. The Prophet (SAW) calls back all those who had gone ahead. He calls forward all the people at the back. He then builds a pulpit from camels' saddles, goes up on it and addresses over 100,000 people in the burning heat of the Arabian Desert, to make an important announcement.

Then the Prophet (SAW) asked just before the declaration, "Do I not have more authority upon you (alastu awla bi kum) than you have over yourselves?" All the people replied, "Yes, surely." Then the Prophet (SAW) declared: "Of whomsoever I am mawla, Ali is also his mawla."

Surely the word "mawla", in this context, refers to authority, to leadership. The earlier reference is from the verse "The Prophet has a greater claim on the faithful than they have on themselves." (Ch.33: V6).[Surah Ahzab]

As Sunni scholar Sibt ibn Jauzi says, "The saying of the Holy Prophet that Ali has authority or is the master over the selves of all the believers clearly proves the Imamate or vicegerency of Ali and that obedience to him is obligatory."

After the declaration, the Prophet (SAW) uttered the following prayer: "O Allah! Love him who loves Ali, and be enemy of he who is the enemy of Ali; help him who helps Ali, and forsake him who forsakes Ali."

This prayer shows that Imam Ali (AS), on that day, was being entrusted with a position that would make some people his enemies and therefore he would need supporters in carrying out his responsibilities. This could not be anything but the position of the mawla in the sense of ruler, master and lord. Are helpers ever needed to carry on or protect a 'friendship' from enemies?

3.1.3 The body language

Sunni scholar Allama ibn Hajar Asqalani narrates in his book, al-Isabah, how the Prophet (SAW) stood next to

Imam Ali (AS) on a raised pulpit or mimbar built from the saddles of camels, raised Ali's hand, his arm in the air, and placed a turban on his head. Now, if that's not a coronation, then what is?

3.2 Common sense

Why would the Prophet (SAW) waste time in the hot Arabian Desert, to tell over 100,000 people that Ali (AS) was his "friend"? Didn't they know that? Wouldn't you be annoyed if you were in that crowd? Why waste everyone else's time, and that too after an exhausting Hajj and in all that heat, unless you have something important to announce?

3.3 Evidence from the Holy Qur'an

Ponder over the Qura'nic verse which was revealed prior to Ghadeer Khumm: "O Messenger! Convey what had been revealed to you from your Lord; if you do not do so, then [it would be as if] you have not conveyed His message [at all]. Allah will protect you from the people." (Ch.5: V67) [Surah Maidah]

Countless classical Ahle Sunnah scholars have said that this verse was revealed ahead of the event of Ghadeer Khumm, perhaps the most famous of all being Imam Fakhruddin al-Razi in his Tafisr al-Kabir.

How can Muslims believe, as the Holy Qur'an warns, that the whole of the Prophet's mission was about to be rendered null and void if he didn't tell the people that he and Ali (AS) were friends? This verse shows how important the announcement was – and how controversial Allah (SWT) knew it would be. The Holy Qur'an says: "Allah will protect you from the people". Why might the Prophet need protecting? Because; the issue of succession was being clarified and confirmed, once and for all, explicitly and publicly, and some people in the crowd were going to be upset and rebellious.

And what happened after the sermon at Ghadeer was over? What verse was revealed? According to all the major classical books of the Ahle Sunnah (Hafiz Jalaluddin as Suyuti, Shaykh Sulayman al-Qandoozi Hanafi, Allama ibn Kathir, among them): "This day have I perfected for you your religion and completed My favour on you and chosen for you Islam as your religion" (Ch.5: V3) [Surah Maidah].

This is the final verse of the Holy Qur'an! And what an occasion it was revealed on!

Again, some common sense is needed: would Allah (SWT) really be unable or unwilling to "perfect" his religion and name it "Islam" unless the issue of the Prophet's "friendship" with Ali was cleared up for the Muslims? This is illogical and an insult to our intelligence! The truth is that Islam was completed and named for the Prophet (SAW) only after the Prophet (SAW) announced Ali (AS) as his successor. Islam wasn't complete until the caliphate of Ali (AS) was announced, revealed, made clear, to the Muslim masses.

Otherwise, you have to believe that that the 22 -year mission of the Prophet (SAW) was being invalidated over the issue of his "friendship" with Ali (AS). And ask yourself this: was it the announcement of a friendship or the appointment of a successor to the Prophet that perfected the religion of Islam? What do you think?

3.4 Second caliph's reaction

It is narrated that after the sermon was over, the Prophet set up a tent with Ali (AS) and the companions lined up to give allegiance (bay'at) to Imam Ali (AS), led by, Umar ibn Khattab, second caliph of the Ahle Sunnah.

According to, among others, Sunni scholars like Imam Fakhruddin al-Razi in his book, and Imam Ahmed ibn Hanbal, in his Musnad, Umar ibn Khattab was the first to arrive on the scene, and looking at Ali, he said: "Well done ibn Abu Talib! Today you became the master of all believing men and women, 'Ameer al-Mo'mineen'!"

This title, Ameer al-Mo'mineen, (Commander of the Faithful), that Shias use today to refer to Imam Ali (AS), and for which they are often condemned and criticised by the Ahle Sunnah, was first used by none other than Umar ibn Khattab. How ironic! Ameer al-Mo'mineen has only one meaning – commander, leader, master of the faithful. When Mullah Umar of the Taliban set up the Islamic Emirate of Afganistan, what did he call himself? Ameer al-Mo'mineen.

Yet we know from Ghadeer Khumm, from the public testimony of Umar ibn Khattab, that the first and only legitimate Ameerul Momineen, appointed by Allah (SWT) via His Messenger, is Ali ibn Abu Talib (AS).

3.5 Imam Ali (AS) invoked Ghadeer later on

Imam Ali (AS) himself offered the event of Ghadeer Khumm, as evidence for his leadership, his caliphate and imamat, later on in his life, after the Prophet's death. There are numerous examples and one of the most famous is as follows: The Sunni scholars ibn Qutaybah, ibn Hanbal, Muttaqi al-Hindi and Abu Nuaym Isfahani, all record in their books that during the caliphate of Ali, (AS) when his authority was being questioned and rebellions were brewing, Imam Ali (AS), in public, said to Anas ibn Malik, the famous companion of the Prophet (SAW): "Why don't you stand up and testify what you heard from the Messenger of Allah on the day of Ghadeer?" Anas answered, "O Ameer al-Mo'mineen! I have grown old and do not remember." To which Ali (AS) responded: "May Allah mark you with a white spot (of leprosy) unconcealable with your turban, if you are intentionally withholding the truth." And when Anas got up from his place he bore a large white spot on his face. From that day onwards, Anas used to say, "I am under the curse of the righteous servant of Allah, Ali ibn Abu Talib!"

The Ghadeer Khumm incident makes it clear that Ali (AS) was the Prophet's successor. But there are other examples from the Prophet's life too. For example, at start of the Prophethood, according to the Tarikh, or History, of Allama Tabari, the famous Sunni historian: The Prophet (SAW) asked three times, at a dinner for his friends and relatives, who will help him in his prophetic mission? On each of the three occassions, only Ali (AS) stood up and said he would. On the first two occasions, the Prophet asked Ali (AS) to sit down. But, on the third occasion, the Prophet said: "Verily this is my brother, my successor, and my caliph amongst you. Therefore, listen to him and obey." Abu Lahab (the Prophet's paternal uncle) said to Abu Talib (his brother and Ali's father) "the Prophet (SAW) has told you to obey your own son!"

The tragedy is that the majority of the Muslims do not understand today what Abu Lahab understood on the first day of the introduction of Islam in Makkah.

Question 4: Why do Shias think Ali (AS) is superior to the first three caliphs?

This is not just a Shia view, that Imam Ali (AS) is superior to the rest of the caliphs and sahabah. A number of Ahle Sunnah scholars and books agree with this view.

4.1 References from books of Ahle Sunnah

Imam Ahmad ibn Hanbal, one of the four Ahle Sunnah Imams of fiqh, said: "There is no Companion about whom as many merits are reported as Ali ibn Abu Talib."

The prominent Ahle Sunnah scholar of India, Shah Ismail Muhaddith Dehlvi, wrote: "Ali al-Murtadha has also an edge over Abu Bakr as-Siddiq and Umar Faruq and this edge lies because of the greater number of his followers and all the highest spiritual and saintly activity, from his days to the end of the world, has to be mediated through him, and he has a say in the kingdom of the kings and the leadership of the leaders and this is not hidden from those who are familiar with the world of sovereignty. Most spiritual chains are directly derived from Ali al-Murtadha. So, on the Day of Judgment, Ali's army, including followers of high status and great reputation, will outnumber and outshine others to be a source of wonder for all the spectators."

In fact, to even compare Ali ibn Abu Talib (AS) with any of the companions is absurd. It is a misunderstanding of who Ali (AS) is, what Ali (AS) represented and stood for. Imam Ali (AS) was on a different level; he wasn't a mere companion like Abu Bakr or Umar or even Ammar and Salman.

4.2 Evidence from the Holy Qur'an

The Sunni scholar Allama Muttaqi al-Hindi, in his famous book, Kanz al-Ummal, narrates a tradition (hadith) from the Prophet (SAW), in which the Prophet (SAW) was asked by a visitor to Madinah to name his favourite companion. When he omits the mention of Imam Ali (AS), he was asked: "But what about Ali? "To which the Prophet (SAW) replied: "Look at this man, he asks me about my own self."

This hadith of course is a reflection of the Ayat of Mubahela of the Holy Qur'an, (Ch.3: V61) [Surah Alay Imran] which states:"But whoever disputes with you in this matter after what has come to you of knowledge, then say: Come let us call our sons and your sons and our women and your women and our selves and your selves, then let us be earnest in prayer, and pray for the curse of God on the liars"

All of the Ahle Sunnah historians, including Muslim in his Sahih, Book 31, Hadith Number 5915, testify that the Prophet (SAW) took Hasan (AS) and Husayn (AS) with him as his "sons", Lady Fatima (AS) with him as the representative of "women", and Imam Ali (AS) as his self, (as his nafs).

The reason why Ali (AS) is not just superior to the rest of the companions, including the first three caliphs is because he went beyond what a companion was: he wasn't just a companion of the Prophet (SAW); he was, as Allah (SWT) says in the Holy Qur'an, and the Prophet (SAW) says in his tradition (hadith), a self of the Prophet, nafs al-Rasoolallah.

Question 5: Why did Ali (AS) not fight for the leadership if it was his God-given right?

Imam Ali (AS) never took up arms against Abu Bakr or Umar or Uthman. Some Ahle Sunnah scholars try and argue that this shows he was not opposed to them. This is an incorrect analysis and a misunderstanding of Imam Ali's (AS) thinking and motivations.

5.1 The reasons

The reason Ali ibn Abu Talib (AS) did not fight after the death of the Prophet (SAW) is because he did not want to divide the nascent, infant Muslim community. He did not want innocent Muslims to die in battle, killing each other, in order to take power. The historians, Sunni and Shia, record how Abu Sufyan offered him troops but Imam Ali (AS) turned him down and criticised his divisive offer.

5.2 His divinely-appointed role as Imam

Imam Ali's (AS) imamat, his caliphate, his wilayat, was given to him by the Prophet (SAW) on the command of Allah (SWT). He was not expected to go and force the Muslims, the people, to follow him; it was their job to find him and follow him. His position as the Imam was not a political or elected position. It was bestowed upon him by Allah (SWT). Kanz al-Ummal, the Sunni book of ahadith, narrates the tradition in which the Prophet (SAW) told Imam Ali (AS): "[O Ali], You are like the Kabah, people go the the Kabah, the Kabah does not come to the people...."

5.3 Common sense

Imam Ali (AS) may not have fought against Abu Bakr and Umar; but he never fought for them either, as part of their armies. Why not? He also refused to give allegiance (bay'at) to Abu Bakr for at least six months after the death of the Prophet and his beloved wife Lady Fatima (AS), who died soon after the Prophet. Why didn't he? The Shias, of course, would also argue that he never pledged any formal allegiance to them at any point in his lifetime. Again, why? What was his problem with them?

This is explained in Nahjul Balagha where Imam Ali (AS) devotes entire sermons to questioning how Abu Bakr and others robbed him of his right to caliph (caliphate) but this is a Shia book. So consider instead the words of Imam Ali ibn Abu Talib (AS) to the six-man committee appointed by Umar on his deathbed to pick a new caliph – and narrated by all of the Sunni ulema.

The committee requested Imam Ali (AS) to take over the position as caliph but on the condition that he abides with the following:

- The Holy Qur'an
- The Prophet's traditions
- The laws and regulations, the "sunnah", introduced by the first two caliphs.

Imam Ali (AS) replied that the first two conditions were acceptable to him but, he had his own views and opinion on the third condition. All of the Sunni historians agree that Imam Ali (AS) rejected the sunnah of Abu Bakr and Umar, upon the death of the latter. Why would he do that if he had accepted the legitimacy of their leadership?

Question 6: Why do Shias refuse to accept that the Prophet (SAW) did not leave a successor?

Some Muslims are of the opinion that the Prophet (SAW) left it to the people to decide. Wouldn't he have written a will if he wanted to leave behind a successor or appoint Imam Ali (AS)?

6.1 Common sense

The idea that the Prophet of Islam who never left Madinah without appointing someone to take charge of the city in his absence, left behind an Islamic state without appointing a successor and without even laying out the rules for how to appoint a successor, is just unbelievable, fanciful and absurd. It is illogical to believe such a thing.

Then there is the issue of the will – or lack thereof. In Islam, making a will is vitally important. The idea that the Holy Prophet (SAW) who told his followers to make sure they left wills behind, when they died, even if they were the poorest of the poor, would die without leaving a will behind is equally absurd – and an insult to the Prophet (SAW).

6.2 References from books of Ahle Sunnah

The truth is that the Prophet did try to make a will but was prevented from doing so by a group of his companions.

According to Sahih Bukhari, Volume 4, Book 53, Hadith Number 393, Said ibn Jubair narrated: I heard Ibn Abbas saying, "Thursday! And you know not what Thursday is? After that Ibn Abbas wept till the stones on the ground were soaked with his tears. On that I asked Ibn Abbas, "What is (about) Thursday?" He said, "When the condition (i.e. health) of Allah's Apostle deteriorated, he said, 'Bring me a bone of scapula, so that I may write something for you after which you will never go astray'. The people differed in their opinions although it was improper to differ in front of the Prophet."

They said, 'What is wrong with him? Do you think he is delirious? Ask him (to understand). The Prophet (SAW) replied, 'Leave me as I am in a better state than what you are asking me to do.' Then the Prophet ordered them to do three things saying, 'Turn out all the pagans from the Arabian Peninsula, show respect to all foreign delegates by giving them gifts as I used to do." The sub-narrator (Said ibn Jubair) added, "The third order was something beneficial which either Ibn Abbas did not mention or he mentioned but I forgot."

How can it be possible that the people who memorized the Holy Qur'an forgot the last, dying instruction of the Prophet (SAW)?

According to this tradition (and others) in Sahih Bukhari the Prophet (SAW) went to write his will but was prevented by a group of his companions, led according to most of the narrations by Umar ibn Khattab, who defied the Qur'anic injunction against raising one's voice in front of the Prophet (SAW) and who accused the Prophet (SAW) of being delirious, of having lost his mind. When the Prophet tried verbally telling them the contents of his will, his final commands, they claim to have forgotten what he said.

Abu Bakr had the foresight to leave behind a will; Umar appointed a six-man election committee – but the Prophet (SAW)? He died without leaving behind any guidance or will… Does this make any sense?

The reason there was no written, public will is because the Prophet (SAW) wanted to write such a document but some of his companions knew he was going to put in writing what he had said at Ghadeer Khumm and so they stopped him from doing so. This important event, this act of rebellion on their part at the deathbed of the Prophet (SAW) is narrated in Sahih Bukhari, in Sahih Muslim, in the Musnad of Imam Ahmed ibn Hanbal and countless other Ahle Sunnah books of ahadith and history.

Question 7: Why is Ali's (AS) name not mentioned in the Holy Qur'an?

There are four responses to this common and provocative question.

7.1 Evidence from the Holy Qur'an

Imam Ali's (AS) name might not be mentioned in the Holy Qur'an but there are countless verses of the Holy Qur'an devoted to the praise of Ali (AS) and to announcing his superiority over the rest of the Muslims, proving his leadership, his wilayat and his imamat.

Allama ibn Hajar Makki, the famous Sunni aalim, quotes the companion and cousin of the Prophet, Abdullah ibn Abbas, saying that he heard from the Prophet (SAW) himself that 300 verses of the Holy Qur'an were revealed specifically in praise of Imam Ali (AS).

For example, the famous verse of the ring: "Your master [wali] can be only Allah; and His messenger and the those who believe, who establish worship and pay the poor rate, and pay the zakat while bowing down (in prayer), in ruku" (Ch.5:V 55) [Surah Maidah] .

Ahle Sunnah and Shia commentators of tafasir unanimously agree that this particular verse refers to Imam Ali ibn Abu Talib (AS), who gave his ring to a beggar while in the state of bowing (ruku) in the the middle of his (salah) prayer, as narrated by Abu Dharr al-Ghafari.

7.2 Importance

Why is it so important to have Imam Ali's (AS) name in the Holy Qur'an? Are we ranking people's importance on whether their name appears in the Holy Qur'an or how many times? If so, then it is worth mentioning that the name of the human being mentioned most in the Holy Qur'an is Prophet Musa (Moses) – 136 times in 34 different chapters (surahs). Then there is Prophet Yusuf (Joseph) mentioned by name 27 times, and Prophet Isa (Jesus) mentioned 25 times.

The Holy Prophet, however, Muhammad (SAW), the Messenger of Islam and the Seal of the Prophets, is mentioned by name just four times, in surah numbers 3, 33, 47 and 48. Are Muslims expected to believe that Musa is higher in status or more important than the Holy Prophet? Or Yusuf is? Or Isa is? This is what happens when you start determining people's status on the crude and arbitrary basis of how many times their name is mentioned in the Holy Qur'an. Allah (SWT) decides in His wisdom whose name appears in His book.

7.3 What if his name had been mentioned?

What if Imam Ali's (AS) name was mentioned in the Holy Qur'an? Would that change anything? Would that change his opponents' minds about the validity and legitimacy of his imamat? Of course not! Those who do not want to follow Imam Ali (AS) would not do so no matter where his name appeared in the Qur'an. After all, the Holy Prophet explicitly said at Ghadeer Khumm: "Of whomsoever I am mawla, Ali is also his mawla". Imagine this sentence as a verse of the Holy Qur'an – how would life be any different? Some would still say it meant friend not leader, others would try and deliberately misrepresent and misinterpret it, or simply ignore it. It's a diversionary tactic to bring up the fact that Allah (SWT) in His Infinite Wisdom decided not to refer to

Imam Ali (AS) by name in the Holy Qur'an, even though He did make around implicit or indirect 300 references to Imam Ali (AS) – as testified by Ibn Abbas.

7.4 Common Sense

Imagine if we extended this argument – Ali (AS) is not the leader because his name isn't mentioned in the Holy Qur'an; Ali (AS) is not important because his name is not explicitly cited in any of the verses of the Holy Qur'an– to the rest of our religious principles, beliefs and obligations. How would we know how to pray morning (Fajr) prayers? Or know that evening (Maghrib) is three units (rakaat) and night (Isha) is four units (rakaat)? The Holy Qur'an doesn't say so; it was left to the Prophet (SAW) to explain the details of the Qur'anic diktats, the Qur'anic commandments.

As the sixth Shia holy Imam Jafar as Sadiq (AS) famously told his companions: "The Qur'an says to pray Fajr salah (morning prayers) but it is the Prophet who tells us that Fajr is two units of prayer (rakatain), the Qur'an tells us to pay zakaat, but it is the Prophet who tells us how to calculate zakaat; in the same way, the Qur'an tells us to obey the "ulul-amr", the people charged with authority, and it is the Prophet who tells us that the "ulul-amr" are: Ali ibn Abu Talib (AS) and the Imams of the Ahlul Bayt."

Question 8: Why do you call yourselves "Shias", or "Shias of Ali", and not just Muslims?

The word "Shia" in Arabic simply means follower, friend, lover, partisan. It is a word that has no negative connotations. In fact it is used in the Holy Qur'an twice with reference to prophets of God.

8.1 Evidence from the Holy Qur'an

Ch.37: V83: "Wa ina min SHIAtehe la Ibrahim" – "And, verily, of among the followers, among the Shias, of Nuh (of Noah), was Ibrahim (Abraham) [Surah Saffat].

Ch.28: V15: "And he (Musa /Moses) went into the city at a time when people (of the city) were not watching, so he found therein two men fighting, one being his Shia – min SHIAtehe - and the other being his enemy, and the one who was his Shia cried out to him for help against the one who was of his enemy." [Surah Kahf].

So Shia is a word used by Allah (SWT) Himself! But these Shias weren't, of course, Shias of Ali (AS). Where does this phrase, "Shia of Ali", come from? It comes from the Prophet's own lips, during the Prophet's own lifetime.

8.2 References from books of Ahle Sunnah

Imam Ahmed ibn Hanbal, Allama ibn Hajar Makki, Hafiz Abu Nuaym Isfahani, and countless other classical scholars of the Ahle Sunnah all narrate that the Prophet said: "Glad tidings, O Ali! Verily you and your companions and your Shia (your followers) will be in Paradise."

Hafiz Jalaluddin al-Suyuti, the famous Ahle Sunnah scholar of Egypt, in his book, al-Durr al-Mansur, narrates a tradition (hadith) in which the companions say: "We were with the Holy Prophet when Ali came towards us. The Holy Prophet said: He and his Shia will acquire salvation on the Day of Judgement."

Allama ibn Hajar Asqalani, another famous Ahle Sunnah scholar of hadith, narrates the following tradition of the Prophet (SAW): "The parable of Ali is like a tree, in which I am the root, Ali is the branch, Hasan and Husayn are the fruits, and the Shias are the leaves."

Allama ibn Hajar al-Haythami al-Makki - of the Ahle Sunnah says in his book al-Sawaiq al-Muhriqa that the Shias are "rafidhi" (liars, deviants) and yet in the same book he narrates a tradition from Abdullah ibn Abbas in which ibn Abbas says that: When the verse: "Those who believe and do righteous deeds are the best of the creation" Ch.98:V7 [Surah Al Bayyina] was revealed, the Messenger of Allah said to Ali: "They are you and your Shia."

He continued: "O Ali! (on the Day of Judgment) you and your Shia will come towards Allah well-pleased and well-pleasing, and your enemies will come angry with their head forced up. Ali said: "Who are my enemies?" The Prophet (SAW) replied: "He who disassociates himself from you and curses you. And glad tiding to those who reach first under the shadow of al-Arsh on the Day of Resurrection." Ali asked: "Who are they, O the Messenger of Allah?" He replied: "Your Shia, O Ali, and those who love you."

Now, here is an important point to consider: some Muslims ask why there is a sect called Shias? They tend to call themselves Sunni Muslims. But where is the word Sunni in the Holy Qur'an or in the ahadith of the Holy Prophet? Where is the hadith in which the Prophet (SAW) refers to his "Sunnis" or even to the "Ahle Sunnah wal Jamaah"? There isn't one. But the Shias have been around since the time of the Prophet (SAW) and Shia is a title of distinction used in the Holy Qur'an.

Question 9: Isn't Shia'ism a product of Abdullah ibn Saba, a Jewish convert to Islam?

9.1 Who is he?

There is a question as to whether Abdullah ibn Saba even existed! In Ahle Sunnah tradition, he was a Yemenite Jew who embraced Islam very late in life. During the time of Ali ibn Abu Talib (AS) he is alleged to have introduced a number of concepts that later were ascribed to both the Shias and the Ghuluww: the exaltation of Ali (AS), his divine appointment by the Islamic Prophet Muhammad (SAW) as a successor, and his alleged divinity. These are all claimed to be concepts that were first formulated and expressed by Ibn Saba and his followers, who are also accused of killing the third caliph of the Ahle Sunnah, Uthman ibn Affan, and dividing the Muslims into two sects.

Yet neutral modern western historians, non-Muslims like Godfrey Hodgson, Leone Caetani, Israel Freidlander and Bernard Lewis have all concluded that he probably did not exist and even if he did, he certainly wasn't responsible for all the intrigues, plots and religious conspiracies that have been attributed to him by some anti-Shia scholars.

9.2 References from books of Ahle Sunnah

Tabari's source for the story of Ibn Saba, Sayf ibn Umar, has been discredited by Imam Hakim, Ibn Hajar Asqalani and several other prominent Ahle Sunnah scholars. In his acclaimed book, "The Succession to Muhammad", former Oxford University professor Wilferd Madelung writes how "few if any modern historians would accept Sayf's legend of Ibn Saba". Note the use of word "legend"!

Even the Egyptian historian, Dr Taha Husayn, one of the most influential Ahle Sunnah scholars of the 20th century, has said that the "fabrication" of Ibn Saba was done by the enemies of the Shias and that the insertion of a "Jewish element" was aimed at discrediting the Shias. He noted that the absence of any record of Ibn Saba being present at the Battle of Siffin suggests that Ibn Saba is a fictitious person.

Question 10: **Why do you give such importance to the father of Ali (AS), Abu Talib? Wasn't he a non-believer?**

Some Muslims not only criticise and reject Ali (AS), they even go after his father. Abu Talib is described as an unbeliever (kafir). Even the recent BBC2 documentary on the life of the Prophet (SAW) presented by Rageh Omaar, stated as a fact that he died as a non-believer.

Yet the following proofs from history and proofs from the Holy Qur'an prove that he was a Muslim.

10.1 He perfomed the Prophet's wedding

Abu Talib performed the wedding ceremony (nikah) of Prophet Muhammad (SAW) and Lady Khadija (AS) and paid the dowry (mahr). How can anyone believe that the wedding ceremony of the Holy Prophet of Islam would be performed by a non-Muslim?

10.2 His marriage

Abu Talib was married to Fatima bint Asad, the mother of Ali (AS) and stayed married to her even after the advent of Islam. If he was a non-Muslim, this would be in defiance of the injunctions contained in the Holy Qura'n.

Even the Prophet's own adopted daughters were divorced from the sons of Abu Lahab (who refused to become Muslims). Fatima bint Asad, remember, was the second lady to accept Islam (after Lady Khadija (AS) the Prophet's first wife).

Imam Sajjad (AS), the fourth Shia Imam, said about his great-great-grandfather: "I wonder why people doubt the faith of Abu Talib, when a woman cannot continue her matrimonial alliance with a non-Muslim husband after she has embraced Islam, and Fatima bint Asad was amongst those women who embraced Islam at a very early stage and still remained his wife till he breathed his last."

10.3 Evidence from the Holy Qur'an

Ch.4:V 144 [Surah Al Nisa], says: "O you who believe! Do not take the unbelievers as protectors instead of the believers" and Ch 9:V 23 [Surah Tawba] proclaims: "O you who believe! Take not for protectors your fathers and your brothers if they love infidelity above Faith: if any of you do so, they do wrong."

The Prophet's grandfather Abdul Muttalib died when he was 8 years old. The Prophet was looked after by Abu Talib (not by his other uncles, Harith or Abbas); from the age of 8 to 25. The Prophet lived under either the direct or indirect care and supervision of his uncle Abu Talib right up until the latter's death in 619 AD, when the Prophet was 49. The Prophet lived under the protection of his uncle, the alleged non-believer, for over 40 years! So was the Prophet (SAW) violating the commands of the Holy Qur'an?

The Holy Qur'an refers to Allah (SWT) and the Prophet, in Ch 93, V 6-9) [Surah Al Duha] : "Did He not find thee an orphan and give you shelter? And He found thee wandering, and He gave thee guidance. And He found thee in need, and made thee independent."

There is no disagreement, as the historical records show, that it was Abu Talib who gave shelter to the Prophet (SAW) took care of all his needs and gave him guidance. Now how is it that in this case Allah (SWT) is taking credit for things that a "kafir" did? How could Allah (SWT) ask for help from a "kafir" in taking care and bringing up His most beloved and final messenger? How could Allah (SWT) do something that He is prohibiting the believers from doing? The fact that the Prophet of Islam took refuge with, and guidance from Abu Talib shows that Abu Talib was not only a Muslim but a mu'min; not just one who submits, but one who believes.

Here is a challenge: can any person, Sunni or Shia, Muslim or non-Muslim, identify even one occasion on which Abu Talib publicly or privately:

- rejected the concept of unity and oneness of Allah (Tawhid)?

- condemned Islam by name, rejected Islam by name and, in doing so, rejected his nephew the Prophet (SAW) of Islam?

- worshipped in front of an idol?

On the contrary, when Muslims pray they should thank Abu Talib, because without him, there would have been no Prophet of Islam and, by extension, no religion of Islam. There is no Muhammad (SAW), without Abu Talib.

CHAPTER 2
THE AHLUL BAYT
(THE PROPHET'S HOUSEHOLD)

Question 11: Doesn't the Ahlul Bayt refer to the wives of the Prophet? Or at least include them?

The phrase Ahlul Bayt, or "people of the household", refers only to certain members of the Prophet's family. The wives of the Prophet (SAW) are excluded from the Ahlul Bayt. How do we know this?

11.1 References from books of Ahle Sunnah

It is narrated in Sahih Muslim that Yazid ibn Hayyan reports from Zayd (a companion of the Holy Prophet), who said: "One day Allah's Messenger (SAW) stood up to deliver a sermon at a watering place known as Khumm situated between Makkah and Madinah. He praised Allah, extolled Him and delivered the sermon and exhorted (us) and said: "O people, I am a human being. I am about to receive a messenger (the angel of death) from my Lord and I, in response to Allah's call, (I bid farewell to you), but I am leaving amongst you two weighty things: the one being the Book of Allah in which there is right guidance and light, so hold fast to the Book of Allah and adhere to it… The second are the members of my household and I remind you (of your duties) to the members of my family."

He (Husayn) said to Zayd: Who are the members of his household? Aren't his wives the members of his family? Thereupon Zayd said: His wives are the members of his family (but here) the members of his family are those for whom acceptance of Zakat (alms and charity) is forbidden." [Book No.31, Hadith no.5920]

In another version of the same tradition (hadith), narrated by Sahih Bukhari:

Zayd says to the Holy Prophet (SAW): "Who are amongst the members of the household? Aren't the wives (of the Holy Prophet) included amongst the members of his household?"

The Prophet (SAW) replied: No, by Allah, a woman lives with a man (as his wife) for a certain period; if he then divorces her and she goes back to her parents and to her people; the members of his household include his ownself and his kith and kin (who are related to him by blood) and for whom the acceptance of Zakat (charity) is prohibited. [Book No.31, Hadith no.5923]

The mention of divorce here is important – not because divorce is a "good thing" or something to be encouraged but because, the Holy Qur'an, in Ch.66: V 4-5, Allah warns two trouble-making wives of the Prophet with divorce: "If he [Muhammad] divorces you, Allah may give him instead wives better than you…" [Surah Al Tahrim].

In Volume 6 of the English translation of Sahih Bukhari, Umar ibn Khattab says it was Aisha bint Abu Bakr and

Umar's own daughter Hafsa who were the wives referred to in the the afore-mentioned Qur'anic verses.

The Prophet (SAW) again and again, in the traditions of the Ahle Sunnah, identifies the Ahlul Bayt as being five people: himself, his daughter Fatima, her husband, Ali ibn Abu Talib, and Hasan and Husayn, the two grandsons of the Prophet. Not just at Ghadeer Khumm or on the Day of Mubahela, when he takes only those four members of his family with him, but on the day the verse, or ayat, of "tathir" (purification) itself was revealed. [Surah Al Ahzab Ch.33: V 33]

It is important here to note that both Sahih Muslim and Sunan Tirmidhi, as well as many other leading Sunni books, confirm this Shia view.

In Sahih Muslim, there is a chapter named "Chapter of Virtues of the Companions". This chapter includes, "Section of the Virtues of the Ahlul Bayt of the Prophet". There exists only one tradition in this section, (hadith number 5955), and this tradition contains no reference to the wives of the Prophet (SAW).

The tradition is known as "The Tradition of the Cloak" or "Mantle" (Hadith al-Kisa), and is narrated by Aisha bint Abu Bakr, wife of the Prophet, as follows:

One day the Prophet (SAW) came out in the afternoon wearing a black cloak (upper garment or long coat), then al-Hasan ibn Ali came and the Prophet accommodated him under the cloak, then al-Husayn came and entered the cloak, then Fatima came and the Prophet entered her under the cloak, then Ali came and the Prophet entered him to the cloak as well. Then the Prophet recited: "Verily Allah intends to keep off from you every kind of uncleanness O People of the House (Ahlul Bayt), and purify you with perfect purification" (the last sentence of Verse in Ch.33:V33) [Surah Al Ahzab].

Note that it is Aisha, the wife of the Prophet (SAW) (and daughter of the first Sunni caliph Abu Bakr) who is the narrator of the above tradition, and she herself is testifying that the Ahlul Bayt are the above-mentioned individuals, and do not include any wives, even her.

Another version of this famous "Tradition of the Cloak" is contained in Sunan Tirmidhi, which is narrated on the authority of Umar ibn Abu Salama, the son of Umm Salama (another wife of Prophet):

The verse "Verily Allah intends to ..." Ch.33:V33 [Surah Al Ahzab] was revealed to the Prophet (SAW) in the house of Umm Salama. Upon that, the Prophet gathered Fatima, al-Hasan, and al-Husayn, and covered them with a cloak, and he also covered Ali who was behind him. Then the Prophet said: "O' Allah! These are the members of my House (Ahlul Bayt). Keep them away from every impurity and purify them with a perfect purification".

"Umm Salama (the wife of Prophet) asked: "Am I also included among them, O Apostle of Allah?" the Prophet replied: "You remain in your position and you are toward a good ending."

11.2 Evidence from the Holy Qur'an

The above verse in Ch.33:V33 [Sura Al Ahzab] known as Ayat of Tathir is very important. It does not refer to the wives of the Prophet, though it appears in a section of verses in which the wives are being discussed.

Those who understand Arabic know that the Holy Qur'an changes subject all the time from verse to verse; also, the gender changes, from feminine to masculine, which refers to a mixed group. It definitely doesn't refer to wives only (as even the Sunni commentator on, and translator of, the Holy Qur'an Abdullah Yusuf Ali admits in his footnote on this verse).

It is also worth mentioning that the Prophet (SAW) did not say: "These are among the members of my House". He said: "These *are* the members of my House". Also note that Umm Salama who is one of the virtuous wives of the Prophet, is the narrator of the tradition to her son and the one who bears witness as to who the Ahlul Bayt are.

The wording of the tradition as narrated by Sunni scholar Imam al-Hakim in volume 2 of his al-Mustadrak makes it quite clear: Umm Salama said: "O Prophet of Allah! Am I not one of the members of your family?" The Holy Prophet replied: "You have a good future but only these are the members of my family. O Lord! The members of my family are more deserving."

Question 12: The Prophet said "I leave two things - the Holy Qur'an and my Sunnah". Why not follow them, rather than the Ahlul Bayt?

It is a common misconception amongst the Ahle Sunnah that the Prophet (SAW) said we should follow the "Holy Qur'an and Sunnah" – especially in his final sermon.

12.1 References from books of Ahle Sunnah

As mentioned earlier, Sahih Muslim in his narration in Book No.31, Hadith No.5920 is very clear in what the Holy Prophet (SAW) said: I am leaving among you two weighty things: the one being the Book of Allah in which there is right guidance and light, so hold fast to the Book of Allah and adhere to it.. . .The second are the members of my household I remind you (of your duties) to the members of my family.

The hadith about the "Holy Qur'an and Sunnah" appears in other Ahle Sunnah books, for example al-Mustadrak (on the authority of Abu Hurayrah) but not in the Sihah Sittah, the six authentic books, of which the two most authentic for the Ahle Sunnah are Sahih Bukhari and Sahih Muslim. And yet, in Sahih Muslim, as we have seen, it clearly states that two things, the two weighty matters, are the Holy Qur'an and the Ahlul Bayt, the Prophet's household.

In Sunan Tirmidhi it says the "two shall not separate from one another until they return to me at the Pool of Paradise". Even if we accept that the Holy Prophet (SAW) referred to Holy Qur'an and his Sunnah – who knew the Prophet's life, his "sunnah", better than anyone else? His family and his household, of course. Those people, like Ali (AS) and Fatima (AS) who were with him from the beginning of his mission; from the revelation of the Holy Qur'an to the boycott in the valley of Abu Talib, to the Battles of Badr, Ohud and Khaybar, to the event of Mubahela and the day of Ghadeer Khumm.

Remember: Shias are those Muslims who follow the Holy Qur'an and Ahlul Bayt, as instructed by the Holy Prophet (SAW) of Islam. Shias do not take one and reject the other; it is a complete package from Allah (SWT) via His Messenger.

Question 13: Where is the concept of Imamat, or Imams, mentioned in the Holy Qur'an?

Most Sunni Muslims refer to the person who lead the congregational prayers (salah) in the local mosque as the "imam". But the word Imam is mentioned in the Holy Qur'an in a number of places and it is worth pondering over some of these verses.

13.1 Evidence from the Holy Qur'an

The Holy Qur'an states: "Yawma naduu kulla unaasim-bi-Imaamihim." "And remember that on the Day of Judgement we will call together all human beings with their respective Imams." Ch.17:V71 [Surah Bani Israel].

"With their respective Imams!" Not with their parents, not with their Prophets, not with their holy books, but with their Imams. That is what the Holy Qur'an says: "with their respective imams". Abdullah Yusuf Ali, however, translates the above verse, verse 71, as, "… we will call them together with their Holy books". However, the verse states "be-imaamihim" not "be-kitaabihim".

The 12th verse of chapter 36 of the Holy Qur'an in Surah Ya Sin, Allah (SWT) says: "Verily it is We who bring the dead to life and keep record of what they have sent forward and left behind; and everything of importance has been vested in the clarifying Imam, the Imam mun Mubeen." (Ch.36: V12)

This verse shows the divinely-mandated importance of the person who is the Imam; it's about much more than just filling a community role and leading the congregational prayers!

Verse 124 of Surah Baqarah, second   chapter (surah) Allah (SWT) says: "And remember when the Lord tried Ibrahim (Abraham) with certain words and he fulfilled them; the Lord said: "Verily I make you an Imam for mankind". (Ch.2:V124)

Imam is a very holy title, a very holy post, or position, explicitly referred to in the Holy Qur'an by Allah (SWT) Himself. Ibrahim (AS) in fact, becomes a prophet first and then an imam; and the the title of imam is bestowed upon him by Allah (SW) after he is "tried" and tested.

Question 14: Why should we believe in 12 Imams, as Shias do?

The reference to the 12 Imams is included in the following books:

14.1 References from books of Ahle Sunnah

Narrated by Jabir ibn Samura: I heard the Prophet (SAW) saying, "There will be twelve Muslim rulers (who will rule all the Islamic world)." He then said a sentence which I did not hear. My father said, "All of them (those rulers) will be from Quraysh." [Sahih Bukhari, Book No.89, Hadith No.329]

"It has been reported on the authority of Jabir ibn Samura who said: I heard the Messenger of Allah (SWT) say: The affairs of the people will continue to be conducted (well) as long as they are governed by twelve men. Then the Holy Prophet said words which were obscure to me. I asked my father: What did the Messenger of Allah (SWT) say? He said: All of the (twelve men) will be from the Quraysh."

And also:

"It has been narrated on the authority of Jabir ibn Samura who said: I heard the Messenger of Allah (SWT) say: Islam will continue to be triumphant until there have been twelve caliphs. Then the Holy Prophet (SAW) said something which I could not understand. I asked my father: What did he say? He said: He has said that all of them (twelve caliphs) will be from the Quraysh." Eight different versions of this hadith are narrated in Sahih Muslim: Book 20, hadith numbers 4477 to 4484.

In fact, there are also countless such traditions (ahadith), referring to twelve caliphs or successors, contained in many other Ahle Sunnah books – Sunan Tirmidhi, Sunan Abu Dawud, Musnad of Imam Ahmed ibn Hanbal, and Kanz al-Ummal.

14.2 The Bible

Then there is the Old Testament of the Bible, in the Book of Genesis, which refers to God speaking to Prophet Abraham (Ibrahim).

"…as for (your son) Ishmael, I have heard you (your prayers): I will surely bless him; I will make him fruitful and will greatly increase his numbers. He will be the father of twelve rulers, and I will make him into a great nation." [Genesis, 17:17-21]

These twelve rulers are often interpreted as being the twelve sons of Ishmael, but even classical Ahle Sunnah scholars like Allama ibn Kathir (whose reference books are best sellers in Saudi Arabia) say it relates to the Holy Prophet's progeny.

Ibn Kathir quotes the Sunni scholar, and forefather of the Wahhabis, Ibn Taymiyah as saying: "And these are the same, regarding whom the Prophet (SAW) has given the glad tidings in the tradition of Jabir ibn Samura and stated their number; indeed this is with regard to the Imams and the Hour will not come till they last."

Indeed Imam Muhammad al-Baqir (AS), the fifth Shia Imam, once said: "We are the remnant of [that] progeny. And that was the prayer of Ibrahim (AS) regarding us."

Question 15: How do we know the 12 Imams are the 12 Shia Imams?

15.1 References from books of Ahle Sunnah

First of all, these traditions (ahadith) are contained in the leading books of Ahle Sunnah scholars. Hence, the burden of proof is on Ahle Sunnah to say who they are, unless Muslims wish to question the prophesy of the Holy Prophet (SAW)! So, who are they?

There is no definite or conclusive response in any of the Ahle Sunnah books.

Ibn Arabi, for example, goes through all of the Ummayad and Abbasid caliphs and concludes: "I cannot understand the meaning of this hadith."

Ibn Hajar Asqalani, a leading Ahle Sunnah scholar and biographer, says: "No one has much knowledge about this particular hadith of Sahih Bukhari."

Hafiz Jalaluddin as Suyuti (a famous Egyptian scholar and Sunni commentator on the Holy Qur'an) has explained as follows: "We see that from the twelve, four are the Righteous Caliphs, then Hasan, then Mu'awiyah, then Ibn Zubayr, and finally Umar ibn Abd al-Aziz. They are eight. Four of them remain."

So where are the 12 names he needs? Suyuti pulls together eight names and then just starts guessing and speculating, in a desperate but unsuccessful attempt to get to 12, as per the prophesy of the Prophet (SAW).

Shias have our 12 Imams and know who the 12 are, by name and lineage.

15.2 Yanabi al-Mawaddah

Some scholars of the Ahle Sunnah have backed the Shias belief in their 12 Imams.

Shaykh Suleman ibn Ibrahim al-Hanafi al-Qandozi states in his book Yanabi al-Mawaddah:

A Jewish man named Na'thal, went to the Prophet (SAW) and said: Every Jewish Prophet left a successor, who is your successor? The Prophet said, specifying them, "After me, Ali ibn Abu Talib and then my two sons, Hasan and Husayn and after Husayn, nine Imams will follow from his children."

"The Jewish man said, 'Name them.'

"The Prophet said, 'When Husayn leaves this world, his son, Ali, and after him, his child Muhammad and after Muhammad, his son Ja'far and after Ja'far, his son Musa and after Musa, his son Ali and after Ali, Muhammad. After Muhammad, his child, Ali and after Ali, Hasan and after Hasan, his child Muhammad al-Mahdi. These are the twelve Imams."

Question 16: Who is this Imam Mahdi (AS) that the Shias believe in and await?

The Shia belief in the Mahdi (AS) is not some unorthodox, unconventional, alien or mystical unIslamic belief. Although, many of the Ahle Sunnah brethren do not know about it or talk about it, all of the three Abrahamic faiths, including Islam (Sunni and Shia), believe in the concept of a messiah, or one who shall return.

16.1 References from books of Ahle Sunnah

In fact, traditions in the Sihah Sittah, the six authentic books of Ahle Sunnah comfirm this point.

Sunan Tirmidhi narrates that the Prophet said, "The world will not come to pass until a man from among my family, whose name will be my name, rules over the Arabs."

Sunan Abu Dawood: "Even if only a day remains for the day of Judgement (Qiyamah) to come, yet Allah (SWT) will surely send a man from my family who will fill this world with such justice and fairness, just as it initially was filled with oppression."

Sunan Ibn Maajah is specific and states: "The promised Mahdi will be among my family."

Sunan Abu Dawood is even more specific: "The promised Mahdi will be among my progeny, among the descendants of Fatima."

The only real or substantive difference between the Shia Mahdi and the Sunni Mahdi is that the Shias believe that the Mahdi is already born, already alive but, in occultation (or "ghaybat"), while Sunni Muslims believe the Mahdi is still to be born.

In fact, the Ahle Sunnah scholars narrate that not only will there be this Mahdi, but he will be different to the Messiah, to Prophet Jesus (Isa), who will also return. It is narrated in Sahih Muslim, the Musnad of Ibn Hanbal and other Sunni books that Prophet Jesus will pray behind the Mahdi. Is it any wonder why the Shias hold their Imams in such high regard?

Question 17: How can a small child become an Imam?

Shias are often criticised for believing in an Imam or leader who was a young boy – Imam Mahdi (AS), after all, was still a small child when his father, the 11th Shia Imam, Hasan al-Askari (AS), was martyred and passed away. The critics claim that such a young Imam would not have the mental capacity to lead the Muslims and be an infallible guide for mankind.

17.1 In response to the non-Muslims:

Why the objection to a brilliant or genius or special child? In the west, child prodigies are accepted and some common examples (accessible via Wikipedia!) include:

- Blaise Pascal (from France) who had mastered Euclidean maths at age 11.

- Jeremy Bentham was fluent in Latin at age of 3.

- John Stewart Mill had a command of Greek at the age of 3.

- Ruth Lawrence entered Oxford in the 1980s at the age of 11 to study maths.

- Kim Ung-Yong, from South Korea, attended university Physics courses at the age of 4 and had obtained a PhD in Physics by the age of 15.

- Akrit Jaswal from India was reading Shakespeare aged 5 and carried out a medical operation aged 7

- Sayid Mohammed Husayn Tabatabai, the Shia prodigy, could recite 60 verses of chapter 30 of the Holy Qur'an at the age of 2. At the age of 5, he could recite the Qur'an from memory (hafidh); and obtained a PhD from Coventry University at the age of 7.

These are all verifiable facts - so why are Shias questioned on the divinely-appointed child prodigy, Imam Mahdi (AS)? No one says that child achievements are impossible or that child prodigies do not exist. Right?

17.2 In response to other Muslims

Why not use the Holy Qur'an as evidence? The following verses very clearly confirm a child can be guided by God: Ch.19: V12 [Surah Maryam]: Allah (SWT) says, about Prophet Yahya, (John the Baptist): "We gave him wisdom and judgment while still a child."

John the Baptist, at least, was a child but what about Prophet Isa (Jesus) who as a baby spoke from the cradle? The Holy Qur'an, describes the birth of Jesus: "O sister of Aaron! Thy father was not a man of evil, nor thy mother a woman unchaste!" But she pointed to the baby. They said: "How can we talk to one who is a child in the cradle?" Ch.19:V 28-34 [Surah Maryam].

Jesus said: "I am indeed a servant of Allah: He hath given me revelation and made me a prophet. . . .And He hath made me blessed wheresoever I be, and hath enjoined on me Prayer and Charity as long as I live; (He) hath made me kind to my mother, and not overbearing or miserable. So peace is on me the day I was born, the day that I die, and the day that I shall be raised up to life (again)."

So youth, childhood, even babyhood, is no barrier to receiving revelation or inspiration from Allah (SWT).

In fact, a number of Shia Imams were very young when they became Imams. The 4th and 11th Shia Imams were in their early twenties, and the 9th and 10th were of ages 7 and 8 respectively when they became Imams upon the deaths of their fathers.

Question 18: How can Imam Mahdi (AS), the 12th Shia Imam, still be alive today? How can he be more than 1,000 years old?

18.1 Scientific facts

Contrary to conventional wisdom, there is nothing in science, which precludes or negates the possibility of such a long life. Human beings are getting older and older – according to Britain's Office of National Statistics (ONS), in 1911: 100 people lived to be over the age of 100 yet in 2007, 9,000 people lived to be over 100!

Dying might be inevitable and unavoidable but ageing isn't – it is a physical process which can be slowed down. One of the world's leading experts in gerontology, former Cambridge University academic Aubrey de Grey has said: "I think the 1st person to live to 1,000 might be 60 already."

Thus, the only difference between the Shias and Aubrey de Grey is that Shias believe that fist person to live to 1,000 is 1,000 already! He is the Imam of our time, the Imam Zamana, Imam Mahdi (AS).

18.2 Evidence from the Holy Qur'an

Muslims who criticise Shias for believing in an Imam who can live till 1,000 years of age should ponder over the verses of the Holy Qur'an.

The Holy Qur'an, after all, says Noah lived till almost a 1,000 years: "Indeed, We sent Noah (Prophet Nuh) to his people, and he tarried among them a thousand years, all but fifty; so the Flood seized them, while they were evil doers." Ch.29:V14 [Surah Ankabut].

The Holy Qur'an also states that Prophet Jesus did not die – but was raised to Heaven: "That they said (in boast), 'We killed Christ, Jesus the son of Mary, the Messenger of God';- but they killed him not, nor crucified him, but so it was made to appear to them, and those who differ therein are full of doubts, with no (certain) knowledge, but only conjecture to follow, for of a surety they killed him not:- Nay, Allah raised him up unto Himself; and Allah is Exalted in Power, Wise." Ch.4:V157–158 [Surah Nisa].

So, Jesus is still alive and yet Sunni Muslims doubt the Shias for believing Imam Mahdi (AS) is alive – despite the fact that Jesus would already have been a thousand years old when the occultation (ghaybat) of Imam Mahdi (AS) began.

And then, of course, there's the Devil: Satan or Shaitan, who was born before Prophet Adam and yet is still with us today; he is a Jinn who has not died. So what we are expected to believe is that Allah (SWT) allows Shaitan to live as long as he likes but Allah (SWT) cannot prolong the life of His representative, His caliphate on earth, Imam Mahdi (AS)? This is nonsensical.

Question 19: How can Shias believe in an Imam that you cannot see?

First, not seeing something does not mean it does not exist. Otherwise, how can we believe in the existence of God?

Then there are the angels and jinns. All Muslims believe in angels that they cannot see, like Gabriel (Jibraeel), the bringer of revelation to Muhammad (SAW). Or how about the Angel of Death? We believe in his existence but we cannot see him in this world.

Again, there's Shaitan too. We cannot see the Devil but we not only believe in his existence but also believe that, despite his 'invisibility', he has the power to do us harm: to manipulate and trick us, to whisper in our ears, as the Holy Qur'an describes in the 114th and final surah of the Holy Qur'an, an-Nas.

Yet, when Shias say they believe in a positive force, a countervailing force, authorised by Allah (SWT), and that this force, this hidden Imam, is alive and available to Muslims as a spiritual (if not a physical) guide, they are accused of being mad, crazy, irrational, weird. Is this fair? Does this make any sense?

Also, it is worth remembering that the occultation or "ghaybat" does not change the status or importance of the 12th Imam, just as the Prophet (SAW) did not stop being the Prophet, nor did the Muslims stop believing in his prophethood, during the Prophet's own enforced disappearance or ghaybat: that is, when the Prophet (SAW) was trapped in a cave for three days while on the way from Makkah to Madinah from during the Hijrah in 622 AD.

Question 20: Why do Shias believe that the Prophet or the Imams are infallible and sinless?

20.1 Evidence from the Holy Qur'an

In Surah Najm, Chapter 53 of the Holy Qur'an, the first five verses state: "By the Star when it sets, Your companion [the Prophet] does not err/wander, nor is he deceived, Nor does he speak out of his desire; It is no less than a revelation that is revealed. The Mighty in Power that has taught him."

The above is very explicit and specific – it is nothing less than a revelation and he doesn't speak out of his own desire. Allah (SWT) is vouching for Him in the Holy Qur'an, so who are we to say or believe otherwise?

Some Ahle Sunnah scholars say the Prophet (SAW) was only infallible on religious issues and that in private he made mistakes. Some Ahle Sunnah books say he forgot to pray on time, or perform correct wudhu (wash), etc, etc. But use your common sense: how would we know that Prophet (SAW) was giving us correct religious information if he was an ordinary, fallible man? Today, how can we be sure that, the morning prayer (Fajr) is three and not two units (rakaat)? If the Prophet (SAW) was fallible, maybe he made a mistake or misremembered when communicating the number of rakaat to his companions. The truth is that infallibility goes hand in hand with prophethood and with all forms of divinely-inspired religious leadership and guidance.

But there are other people, besides the Holy Prophet (SAW), who are also infallible. After all, what does Iblis or Shaitan say, as quoted in the Holy Qur'an,? In Surah Hijr, Ch.15:V 39-40: He said: "My Lord! Because Thou hast sent me astray, I verily shall adorn the path of error for them in the earth, and shall mislead them every one of them. Save such of them as are Thy perfectly devoted slaves."

Aha! According to the Holy Qur'an, not only is the Prophet (SAW) protected from sin and error but there is a group of "perfectly devoted slaves" who even Shaitan admits he cannot mislead or trick. Who are they?

20.2 References from books of Ahle Sunnah

According to Sunni scholars Tirmidhi in his Sunan, ibn Hanbal in his al-Musnad and Hakin in his al-Mustadrak state:

"The Messenger of Allah (SAW), from the time the revelation of "Verily Allah intends to... (the last part of Ch.33:V33)" and for six months thereafter, stood by the door of the House of Fatima (AS) (his daughter) and said: "Time for Prayer Ahlul Bayt; No doubt! Allah wishes to remove all abomination from you and make you pure and spotless."

According to the companion and cousin of the Prophet, Abdullah ibn Abbas: "The Messenger of Allah recited "Verily Allah intends to keep off from you every kind of uncleanness O' People of the House (Ahlul Bayt), and purify you a perfect purification". . . and then the Messenger of Allah (SWT) said: "Thus Me and my Ahlul Bayt are clear from sins." [al-Durr al-Mansur, by Hafiz Jalaluddin al-Suyuti, vol.5, under the commentary of Verse Ch.33:V33 of Holy Qur'an – Surah Al Ahzab]

Case closed.

CHAPTER 3
THE COMPANIONS AND MISCELLANEOUS ISSUES

Question 21: Are Shias hostile to all the companions (the "sahabah")?

21.1 Definition of companions

The majority of the Muslims are obsessed with the companions, (sahabah) – but who are they exactly? How many of them are there? There is no point in Ahle Sunnah falsely accusing Shias of cursing or rejecting all the companions, if we cannot first agree on who the true companions of the Holy Prophet were.

Allama Ibn Hajar Asqalani, the Sunni scholar, writes in his famous book al-Isabah: "Every one who has narrated a hadith or a word from the Prophet, or seen him while believing in him, is counted among the Sahabah. Also, (the sahabah) is any one who has met the Prophet (SAW) while believing in him, and died as a Muslim, whether his meeting with him being long or short, narrating from him or not...or who has seen him without sitting with him, or has not seen him due to an excuse."

This is a very, very wide definition and "companions" defined in this broad and loose way could number more than 100,000 people!

In fact, some Sunni Muslim scholars even include their children as sahabah as well. How can all these "companions" be accepted as being beyond scrutiny? How can anyone accept that all such companions were rightly guided and made no mistakes.

The word itself, sahaba or companion, has become a label of distinction, of nobility and honour. But there is nothing holy or pure about the title 'companion'; it has been elevated beyond its meaning.

21.2 Evidence from the Holy Qur'an

For example, the word is mentioned in the Holy Qur'an in the following verses: Surah Zukhruf, Ch.43:V 36: "And whoever turns himself away from the remembrance of the Beneficent Allah, We appoint for him a Qareen, (a devil, a shaitan), so he becomes his associate, his comrade, his intimate companion."

According to Islam's holy book, your own personal shaitan is called a companion.

Then there is the story of Prophet Yusuf (Joseph), contained in Surah Yusuf, where the latter, while in prison, questions the disbelief and idolatry of two fellow prisoners: "O my two companions of the prison! (I ask you): are many lords differing among themselves better, or is the One Allah, Supreme and better?" Ch.12:V 39 [Surah Yusuf].

The Holy Qur'an mentions the following three types of companions:

21.2.1 The good

Ch.48:V 29 [Surah Fateh]: "Muhammad is the Messenger of Allah; and those who are with him are strong against the unbelievers, (but) compassionate amongst each other. Thou wilt see them bow and prostrate themselves (in prayer), seeking Grace from Allah and (His) Good Pleasure. On their faces are their marks, the traces of their prostration."

These are companions that Shias have no problem with and no objection to. Indeed, these are companions that Muslims today, Sunni and Shia, should adore and try and emulate. Men like Abu Dharr al-Ghafari, Ammar ibn Yasir and Salman Farsi.

Allama Ibn Hajar Makki, the Sunni scholar, narrates that the Prophet (SAW) said, "Verily, Allah has commanded me to love four persons and has told me that He loves them." When the people asked who these four persons were, he said: "Ali ibn Abu Talib, Abu Dharr, Miqdad, and Salman."

Sunan Tirmidhi: "The blue sky has not sheltered, nor has the earth borne a man more honest than Abu Dharr; he lives upon earth with the same austerity and simplicity since the days of Isa ibn Maryam [Jesus, son of Mary]."

Such sahabah are respected and admired by all Shias, who have no objections in following them, quoting them and emulating their behaviour.

21.2.2 Not so good

Ch. 9:V38 [Surah Baraat]: "O you who believe! What is the matter with you, that when ye are asked to go forth in the Cause of Allah, ye cling heavily to the earth? Do you prefer the life of this world to the Hereafter?"

Ch. 49: V2 [Surah Al Hujarat]: "O you who believe! Do not raise your voices above the voice of Prophet ... lest your deeds become null while you do not perceive."

The companions referred to here are those who were Muslims but did not always follow the rules and/or did not always follow the Prophet (SAW). History is full of such examples:

- When the Treaty of Hudabiya was signed, the second caliph Umar and others were reluctant to agree to the treaty and questioned the Prophet's judgement. From Sahih Bukhari: "Umar ibn Khattab said, 'I went to the Prophet and said, "Aren't you truly the messenger of Allah (SWT)?" The Prophet said, "Yes, indeed." I said, "Isn't our cause just and the cause of the enemy unjust?" He said, "Yes." I said, "Then why should we be humble in our religion?" He said, "I am Allah's (SWT) messenger and I do not disobey Him, and He will make me victorious.'" [Sahih al-Bukhari, Volume 3, Book 50, No. 891]

- During the battle of Ohud, a number of leading companions fled the battlefield, leaving the Prophet (SAW) on his own. Their names appear in the history books, both Muslim and non-Muslim and include the first and second caliphs of the Ahle Sunnah.

- As has been discussed on the previous pages, before he died, the Holy Prophet (SAW) asked for a pen and paper to write a will. The companions did not oblige to this request and raised their voices of his, upsetting and angering him. He asked them to leave his room.

21.2.3 The hypocrites

There is a whole chapter in the Holy Qur'an addressed to such "companions": Surah Al-Munafiqun, "The Hypocrites" "When the hypocrites come to you, O' Prophet, they say: "We bear witness that you are the Messenger of Allah." Allah knows that you are His Messenger and Allah bears witness that the hypocrites are liars. They have made their oaths as a shield and turn people away from Allah. Evil indeed is what they do!" Ch. 63: V3 [Surah Al-Munafiqun]]

Read and ponder over the verse in this chapter. Who is Allah (SWT) referring to? Some ask: why did the Prophet (SAW) not identify these evil hypocrites? The Holy Qur'an replies: "And of the people of Madinah are those who are bent on hypocrisy. You know them not, but we know them. Twice we will punish them, and then they will be case into severe punishment." Ch. 9: V:101 [Surah Baraat].

21.3 References from books of Ahle Sunnah

It isn't just the Holy Qur'an but the ahadith, which refer to the hypocrites around the Prophet (SAW), whom the Prophet (SAW) was unaware of! "Some men from my companions will come to me by the Fountain and they will be driven away from it, and I will say, 'O Lord, my companions!' It will be said, 'You have no knowledge of what they innovated after you left: they turned apostate as renegades (reverted from Islam)." [Sahih Bukhari, volume 8, book 76, Tradition 586]

Sahih Bukhari narrates several versions of this particular hadith, Volume 8, Book 76: 578, 585, 586, 587 and 592, translated by Mohammed Muhsin Khan and available, in full, in English, online.

Question 22: Why don't Shias follow all the companions? What about the "hadith of the stars"?

The famous Sunni tradition says: "Verily, my companions are like the stars (nujum) in the sky; whichever of them you follow, you shall be guided rightly."

The authenticity of this hadith is questioned by many Sunni scholars, including Imam Ahmed ibn Hanbal, the founder, of one of the four main Sunni schools of fiqh and law, but let us not dwell on this. Instead, let us use our common sense. After all, history tells us that the various companions fought each other in various battles, after the death of the Prophet – including the battles of Siffin and Jamal.

So, if some Muslims say we have to "unite "around the companions, the response is: which companions? How do we unite around Imam Ali (AS) and Muawiya ibn Abu Sufyan, when the latter went to war against the former at Siffin?

How do we follow both Abu Dharr and Uthman ibn Affan, the third caliphate of the Ahle Sunnah, when the latter had the former beaten and exiled from Madinah after Abu Dharr accused Bani Ummaya of corruption and excess?

Muslims today should unite around the Holy Qur'an and the Ahlul Bayt, not around the various companions, good, not-so-good and hypocritical, who could not even unite themselves.

Question 23: Why do the Shias criticise Aisha, wife of the Prophet?

There is no denying the fact that Shias are hostile towards Aisha bint Abu Bakr, the wife of the Prophet who is often described as "Ummul Momineen," mother of the believers.

23.1 Aisha must be respected

However, most educated Shias do not believe in abusing the name or reputation of Aisha not just because she is someone of great importance to our Sunni Muslim brethren but because she was, whether we like it or not, a wife of the Holy Prophet. Even in the Battle of Jamal, when she went to war with Imam Ali (AS), the latter treated her with respect. He sent her half-brother Muhammad ibn Abu Bakr to catch her when she fell from her camel, after Malik Ashtar had cut off it's hind legs. Imam Ali (AS) did not humilate Aisha - so who are we to curse and humilate her?

23.2 Battle of Jamal

Nonetheless, it is because of events like the Battle of Jamal that we Shias will always be opposed to Aisha and critical of her actions. Shias are those who follow the Holy Prophet (SAW). And what did he say at Ghadeer Khumm? The Prophet (SAW) declared: "O Allah! Love him who loves Ali, and be enemy of he who is the enemy of Ali; help him who helps Ali and forsake him who forsakes Ali."

How can we then love, respect or admire a woman who chooses to become an enemy of Ali? Who tries to persuade others to "forsake" Ali? The fact that she was married to the Holy Prophet is irrelevant here; the issue is whether or not she obeyed the Prophet (SAW) and adhered to the truth.

Taha Husayn, the famous Egyptian Sunni scholar, in his book 'Ali wa banuh' (Ali and His Sons), tells the story of a man during the Battle of Jamal (Battle of Camel) who is confused as to which of the two sides is in the right. He says to himself, "How is it possible that such personalities as Talha and Zubair should be at fault?" He tells Imam Ali ibn Abu Talib (AS) about his dilemma and asks him whether it is possible that such great personalities and men of established repute should be in error. Imam Ali ibn Abu Talib (AS) answers him: "You are seriously mistaken and reversed the measure! Truth and falsehood are not measured by the worth of persons. Firstly find out what is truth and which is falsehood, then you will see who stands by truth and who with falsehood."

Sadly, the Ahle Sunnah scholars these days tend not to engage in the debate around the rights and wrongs of the Battle of the Camel. They maintain that the Prophet told us to follow all his companions, because they are like stars, but cannot explain or justify how "stars" like Talha and Zubayr went up against a star like Ali ibn Abu Talib (AS)? And what was the widow of the Holy Prophet doing on the battlefield, fighting Ali (AS) and leaving her house to do so, despite the Holy Qur'an saying in Surah Ahzab (Ch.33 V:33) that the wives of the Prophet should "stay quietly in their houses"?

It is a rather simple question: which of them was correct at Jamal? Ali (AS) or Aisha? Who was right and who was wrong? It is illogical, irrational and disingenuous to claim that both were "right".

One Sunni researcher, Ather Khan, an aide to Dr Zakir Naik of India, has claimed that "the Battle of Jamal that was fought between the Mother of the Believers, Aisha and Ali. took place as a result of difference of opinion on a political issue. We respect and revere both the companions of the Prophet (SAW). However, with regards to the Battle of Jamal, we neither favour one nor are we against the other."

This is an abdication of moral responsibility. How can you avoid taking a position? What about the people, the Muslims on both sides, killed in that fateful battle? According to the Western historian William Muir at least 10,000 people died in the Battle of Jamal. Others estimate the death toll to be 20,000 or so. What will these souls be told on the Day of Judgement when they are resurrected? Were they on the right side or wrong side? Did they die in vain?

The fundamental fact is: Aisha took up arms against Ali ibn Abu Talib (AS), despite the Prophet (SAW) warning against such a move. And if some Ahle Sunnah scholars of the Wahhabi or Salafi variety in places like Saudi Arabia and Pakistan today can criticise Imam Husayn (AS) for going against Yazid ibn Muawiya, the self-proclaimed caliph, how can they try and silence Shias who try and point out how Aisha bint Abu Bakr wrongly took up arms against Imam Ali (AS), about whom the Holy Prophet (SAW) said: "Love him who loves Ali, and be the enemy of he who is the enemy of Ali", and in doing so caused the deaths of between 10,000 and 20,000 Muslims.

23.3 References from books of Ahle Sunnah

In fact, such was her enmity, her hatred for Imam Ali (AS) that the famous and classical Sunni historian Allama Tabari writes, in the History of al-Tabari Volume 17, page 224 (English translation), that Aisha was delighted when the news of Imam Ali's (AS) death in the mosque of Kufa reached her in 661 AD.

One last tradition worth mentioning on the subject of the Battle of Jamal and the "Mother of the Believers", Aisha bint Abu Bakr, comes from the Sunni book al-Iqd al- Fareed, in which it is narrated: "After the battle of Jamal a woman comes to Aisha and asked her: 'What shall be the punishment if a woman murders her child?' (Aisha) replied: 'The fire'. Then the woman asked: 'What is the punishment [then] for a woman that kills twenty thousand of her children at one place?' (Aisha), angry and outraged, said: 'How dare she say this? Arrest and apprehend this enemy of Allah."

Question 24: Why don't Shias respect Muawiya ibn Abu Sufyan?

There are many reasons that explain and justify the Shia hostility and hatred towards Muawiya. Here are just three of them:

24.1 He killed Imam Hasan (AS)

Muawiya was the man who had the Prophet's grandson Imam Hasan (AS) poisoned and killed. This is a historical fact: more than a dozen of the most famous, most respected classical scholars and historians of the Ahle Sunnah – including Ibn Abdul Barr, Zamakshari, Abul Fida and Masudi – write that Muawiya offered Juda, wife of Imam Hasan, 100,000 dirhams, as well as his son Yazid's hand in marriage, as a reward for poisoning the second Shia Imam, which she agreed to do.

24.2 He killed Ammar ibn Yasir

Muawiya was the man, the "rebel", who the Prophet prophesied would kill the famous companion Ammar ibn Yasir.

Sahih Muslim, Book 41 Hadith, 6966: "Allah's Messenger (SAW) said to Ammar as he was digging the ditch (on the occasion of the Battle of the Ditch) wiping over his head: O son of Summayya you will be involved in trouble and a group of rebels will kill you."

There are four more such ahadith in Sahih Muslim: numbers 6967 to 6970. And classical Sunni scholars Allama ibn Hajar Asqalani and Hafiz Jalaluddin as-Suyuti have both written that this hadith is mutawaatir, which means there can be no doubt about its chain of narration, it is 100% authentic.

So, if any more conclusive historical proof was needed to show the infidelity and hypocrisy of Muawiya then this particular authentic hadith is it. No historian, Sunni or Shia, Muslim or non-Muslim, denies the fact that Ammar was killed by none other than Muawiya in the Battle of Siffin, which was launched by Muawiya and his Syrian army against Imam Ali (AS) and his allies.

The famous and contemporary English translator of Sahih Muslim, Abdul Hamid Siddiqui, has written in the footnote of his translation of this hadith that not only was Ammar killed in the Battle of Siffin but he goes on to add that "this hadith is clearly indicative of the fact that in the conflict between Hazrat Ali and his opponents, Hazrat Ali was on the right as Ammar ibn Yasir was killed in the Battle of Siffin fighting in the camp of Hazrat Ali."

Ironically, a desperate and conniving Muawiya recognized the damage done to his status and standing from the death of Ammar and the prediction of the Prophet (SAW). He subsequently tried to claim that Imam Ali (AS) was to blame for Ammar's death as it was he who had brought Ammar to fight in the Battle of Siffin in his army. Imam Ali (AS), however, reminded the people that if that was the case, then the Prophet of Islam was to blamed for the death of his uncle Hamza as it was the Prophet (SAW) who had brought Hamza to fight in the Battle of Ohud!

24.3 He began the cursing of Ali ibn Abu Talib (AS)

According to Sunan Tirmidhi, the Holy Prophet (SAW) once said: "Loving Ali is the sign of belief, and hating Ali is the sign of hypocrisy."

And the companions are quoted by Tirmidhi as saying:"We used to identify the hypocrites by their hatred for Ali."

Yet Muawiya not only fought against Imam Ali (AS), at Siffin, he cursed Imam Ali (AS) as well and demanded, during his rule of the ummah, that everyone who spoke from the pulpit (mimbar) curse Ali (AS) also. To prove it, let us begin with Sahih Muslim, Book 31, Tradition 5915:

Sa'd ibn Abu Waqqas narrated that: Muawiya, the son of Abu Sufyan, gave order to Sa'd, and told him: "What prevents you that you are refraining from cursing Abu Turab (nickname of Imam Ali)?" Sa'd replied: "Don't you remember that the Prophet said three things about (the virtue of) Ali? So I will never curse Ali."

Hafiz Jalaluddin as Suyuti, the Egyptian Sunni scholar, narrates in al-Durr al-Mansur: "That it was in the days of Bani Umayyah, there were more than seventy thousand pulpits (mimbar) in mosques upon which they cursed Ali ibn Abu-Talib - Muawiya made it a sunnah for them."

Allama Shibli Numani, the dean of India's Sunni historians, writes in his famous biography of Prophet Muhammad, Sirat-un-Nabi: "Among all those extraneous forces which affect and influence the writing of history, none is more powerful than the government...For full 90 years, from Sind in India (Indo-Pakistan) to Asia Minor and Andalusia in Spain, Ali and the children of Fatima were cursed from every pulpit in every mosque after every Friday sermon. Thousands and thousands of hadith glorifying Muawiya, were manufactured, and were put into circulation."

This official media bias, this propaganda, this demonization of Ali (AS) is what created the conditions for the later massacre of the Prophet and Ali's (AS) family at Kerbala, and what set the tone for the humiliations of the Prophet's granddaughters at the hands of Muawiya's son, Yazid, in the court of Damascus in 680 AD.

Rememebr: hatred of the Prophet's household, his Ahlul Bayt, did not appear overnight: it came from Muawiya, who was in power for almost two decades.

Question 25: Why don't Shias accept Abu Hurayrah's traditions?

The "companion" Abu Hurayrah is one of the key sources for the traditions contained in the books of the Ahle Sunnah. The Shias reject him and his traditions for the following reasons:

25.1 Content

Perhaps the major reason why Abu Hurayrah is rejected and shouldn't be trusted is because of the bizarre and often offensive content of the ahadith which are ascribed to him. For example, the ludicrous story of Prophet Musa (Moses) and the stone, from Sahih Bukhari, Volume 1, Book 5, Number 277:

Narrated by Abu Hurayrah: The Prophet (SAW) said, "The (people of) Bani Israel used to take baths naked (all together) looking at each other. The Prophet Moses used to take a bath alone. They said, 'By Allah! Nothing prevents Moses from taking a bath with us except that he has a scrotal hernia.' So once Moses went out to take a bath and put his clothes over a stone and then that stone ran away with his clothes. Moses followed that stone saying, 'My clothes, O stone! My clothes, O stone!' till the people of Bani Israel saw him and said, 'By Allah, Moses has got no defect in his body.' Moses took his clothes and began to beat the stone." Abu Hurayrah added, "By Allah! There are still six or seven marks present on the stone from that excessive beating."

Are we really supposed to believe such nonsense? About Prophet Musa?

25.2 Internal contradictions in his ahadith

Abu Hurayrah said: "Once I entered the house of Ruqayya, the Prophet's daughter and Uthman's wife. She had a comb in her hand. She said: "The Prophet left just a little while ago. I combed his hair. He said to me: "How do you find Abu Abdullah (Uthman)?" I said: "He is good." He said to me: "Grace him! He is the most similar to me, among my companions, in morals."

Now Imam al-Hakim, famous Ahle Sunnah transmitter of ahadith, narrates this and says: "This tradition has a true series of narrators but untrue text, [the content is untrue] because Ruqayya had died in the third year of hijra during the battle of Badr, whereas Abu Hurayra came and became a Muslim after the battle of Khaybar [four years later]." So how did Abu Hurayrah have this conversation that he claims? One which helped the third caliphate Uthman's reputation, conveniently?

25.3 Common sense

Abu Hurayrah narrated over 5,000 traditions after converting to Islam in 629 AD, just three years before the death of the Holy Prophet (SAW).

Can it be possible to accept that such a large number of traditions were narrated by this single person in such a short space of time? And could an illiterate and uneducated man, late to became a Muslim and therefore late in the period of his companionship with the Holy Prophet (SAW) narrate more traditions and sayings from the Prophet than his wives, relatives and lifelong friends and companions?

Remember: he narrated more than 5,000 ahadith in this

time. Compare this with the far fewer ahadith narrated by Aisha, Abu Baker, or Umar and the rest.

In fact, in his book, "Hadith Literature: It's Origin, Development, & Special Features", the Sunni writer Muhammed Zubayr Siddiqui sets out the following details:

- Abu Hurayrah narrated : 5,374 hadiths

- Aisha Umm al-Mo'mineen: 2,210 hadiths

- Umar ibn Khattab : 537 hadiths

- Ali ibn Abu Talib (AS) : 536 hadiths

- Abu Bakr al-Siddiq : 142 hadiths

Excluding Abu Hurayrah, that is a total between them of 3,425. Abu Hurayra narrated more ahadith than all of them put together!

Can any sensible or impartial person believe that Abu Hurayrah, despite his obscurity, his illiteracy and his lack of time alongside the Holy Prophet (SAW), managed to somehow narrate more traditions than the first four caliphs, with all their status, their authority, their presence alongside the Prophet (SAW) during his 22-year mission and their high profile in the decades following his death in 632 AD? Is this what we are expected to believe? It just isn't plausible.

25.4 Companions' testimony

Consider the verdict of Umar ibn Khattab on Abu Hurayrah: Allama Muttaqi al-Hindi in his Kanzul Ummal reports that when he was caliph, Umar lashed Abu Hurayrah, rebuked him and forbade him to narrate ahadith from the Holy Prophet. When asked why he did so, Umar said: "Because you narrate hadith in [such] large numbers from the Holy Prophet, you are fit only for attributing lies to him. So you must stop narrating hadith from the Prophet, otherwise, I will send you back to your tribe in Yemen."

Then there's the verdict of Aisha: Sunni scholars Ibn Qutayba, Hakim and al-Dhahabi say that Aisha repeatedly contradicted Abu Hurayrah and said, "Abu Hurayra is a great liar who fabricates hadith and attributes them to the Holy Prophet."

Allama Ibn Qutayba records the story of Aisha telling Abu Hurayrah: "You tell ahadith about the Prophet Muhammad that we never heard them from him" He answered; "You (Aisha) were busy with your mirror and make up" She (Aisha) answered him; "It is you who were busy with your stomach and hunger. Your hunger kept you busy, you were running after the people in the alleyways, begging them for food, and they used to avoid you and get away from your way, and finally you would come back and pass out in front of my room and the people think you were crazy and step all over you."

In fact, Imam al-Hakim counted up those who narrated traditions from Abu Hurayrah. He found that 28 leading companions, including Imam Ali (AS), Umar, Uthman, Talha and Zubayr were not among them.

But Abu Hurayrah had a huge impact on the history and direction of Islam. Ahle Sunnah Islam, in fact, is built on his narrations, many of them false, unreliable, odd, offensive and contradictory. There is nothing wrong or objectionable with Sunnis calling themselves the followers of the sunnah, but it depends which sunnah. The sunnah as interpreted and narrated by an unreliable narrator who spent less than three years with the Prophet; or the sunnah as interpreted and narrated by a man like Ali ibn Abu Talib (AS) who grew up in the lap of the Prophet, in the home of Prophet and who was by his side from the very first day, from the very first invitation to the Quraysh to join Islam, to the moment he passed away with his head in Imam Ali's (AS) lap.

Question 26: Why don't Shias accept Sahih Bukhari and the authentic Ahle Sunnah collections of ahadith?

26.1 Content

Some of the ahadith in Bukhari are shocking, including many of the ones from Abu Hurayrah cited earlier. Not only are physical attributes ascribed to Allah (SWT); for example, Allah puts His foot in Hell (!), but what is said about the Holy Prophet (SAW) is too disgusting and defamatory and sickening to repeat here in detail. It is sufficent to say that there are traditions contained in Sahih Bukhari which relate to the Prophet (SAW) falling asleep and forgetting the prayer time, forgetting to perform the necessary ablution (wudhu) for prayer, sitting with Aisha to watch a dance with music; taking off his clothes and being naked in public; and discussing his nightly sexual activities with his wives with his companions. These are outrageous claims and slurs that Muslims today would not tolerate from Danish cartoonists or from Salman Rushdie yet we tolerate such offensive nonsense from the supposedly "sahih" book of Bukhari. Why?

The irony is that if Bukhari were alive today, and published his book now containing the claims that it does about the Holy Prophet of Islam, those same Ahle Sunnah scholars who praise him would be the first to issue fatwas declaring him an apostate and ordering for him to be excommunicated and/or killed.

Indeed, by any objective assessment, how can one say that Salman Rushdie is guilty of defaming the Prophet and "Imam" Bukhari is not?

26.2 Bukhari's agenda:

Of his 7,000 or so ahadith, Bukhari narrates around 1,100 ahadith from Abu Hurayrah, roughly the same number from Abdullah ibn Umar and 900 from Anas ibn Malik. None of these three men can be considered front-rank or long-standing or senior companions, by Sunni or Shia standards. What kind of book of "sahih", or authentic and correct, hadith from the Prophet does not narrate from the person who was described by the Holy Qur'an and the Prophet himself as the "self of the Prophet", the "nafs" of the Prophet? How could he claim to be compiling sayings of the Prophet without narrating from the gateway to the knowledge of the Prophet, as Ali (AS) was once so famously referred?

He also failed to narrate traditions from other Imams who you might expect him to have quoted from, like Imam Baqir (AS) and Imam Sadiq (AS), the 5th and 6th Imams of the Ahlul Bayt and well-known for their scholarship and knowledge of the Prophet's traditions.

And it wasn't just Imam Sadiq (AS) that Bukhari refrained from taking ahadith from: he did not take any from four of the Ahlul Bayt Imams who were actually alive during his lifetime: Imam al-Ridha (AS), Imam at-Taqi (AS), Imam an-Naqi (AS) and Imam al-Askari (AS).

Why is Sahih Bukhari devoid of ahadith narrated by these Imams? Or from Ali ibn Abu Talib (AS), despite the Prophet (SAW) saying that the two weighty things he was leaving us with were the Holy Qur'an and his Ahlul Bayt, his household? Can you then blame the Shias for rejecting the so-called Sahih Bukhari?

Question 27: What is "taqiyah"? Is it not lying, deception and deceit?

"Taqiyah" means dissimulation: concealing or disguising one's beliefs or intentions.

Today, lots of Islamophobes and Muslim-haters say the traditional Shia belief in Taqiyah makes us Muslims, Sunni and Shias alike, dishonest, untrustworthy people. Yet nothing could be further from the truth. Islam takes a hard line against lying in general, and stresses the importance of truth and honesty. But like every other ethical system on earth, whether religious or secular, there are certain exceptions to rules in certain, often extreme scenarios.

So, if your life is at risk, or your family's life is at risk, you are allowed to conceal the fact that you are a Muslim – just as, for example, the Jews tried to conceal their faith from the Nazis in the 1930s and 1940s to avoid being sent to the Nazi gas chambers.

Taqiyah is a form of self-defence, of self-preservation and it is referred to in the Holy Qur'an and the books of the Ahle Sunnah.

27.1 References from books of Ahle Sunnah

Imam Fahkruddin Razi, one of the greatest of classical Ahle Sunnah scholars, writes in his famous Tafseer al-Kabeer, volume 4: "Taqiyyah is permissible till the day of Qayamah...because it is Wajib (compulsory) to protect our life from any harm."

In fact, he goes even further than this and writes: "Taqiyyah is permissible for self protection, but is it permissible for the protection of wealth?" he asks. Your property? Your money? Your wealth and income? "It probably is permissible," he concludes.

27.2 Evidence from the Holy Qur'an

Forget for a moment the verdicts of the Sunni and Shia scholars; look at the verdict of Allah (SWT). The key verse from the Holy Qur'an which states: "Anyone who, after accepting faith in Allah (SWT), utters disbelief (save under compulsion and even then his heart remains firm in faith) on them is Wrath from Allah (SWT) and theirs will be a dreadful Penalty." Ch.16: V:106 [Surah An-Nahl].

All Muslim scholars agree that this verse descended in relation to the suffering of Ammar ibn Yasir at the hands of the Quraysh in Makkah. Allamah Hafiz Jalaludeen as Suyuti of Egypt, in his commentary on this verse states: "The non-believers once caught Ammar ibn Yasir and they forced him to praise their false gods and to condemn Prophet Muhammad (SAW). They forced him to an extent that Ammar ibn Yasir gave in, and conceded to their demands. After that, when he returned to the Prophet Muhammad (SAW), Ammar narrated the whole story to him. The Prophet (SAW) asked him:

"How do you feel in your heart?" To which Ammar replied: "I am fully content with Allah's religion in my heart". To this the Prophet (SAW) said: "If non-believers ask you to say the same again, say it". Then the following verse (ayat) was revealed:

"Anyone who, after accepting faith in Allah, utters disbelief (save under compulsion and even then his heart remains firm in faith) on them is Wrath from Allah and theirs will be a dreadful Penalty". [Surah Al Nahl - Ch.16:V106]

There are several other verses of the Holy Qur'an which speak of the importance and legitimacy of taqiyah if the situation demands it: one example worth noting is from Ch.12: V: 4-5 [Surah Yusuf]: "When Yusuf said to his father: O my father! Surely I saw eleven stars and the sun and the moon - I saw them bowing down to me. "He said: O my son! Do not relate your vision to your brothers, lest they devise a plan against you; surely the Shaitan is an open enemy to man."

Here, Prophet Jacob (Yaqub) is telling Prophet Joseph (Yusuf) to do taqiyah with his own brothers. Why? Because he's worried they'll turn against him and try and get rid of him – which is what they then do when they discover the truth!

27.3 Common sense

Taqiyah isn't lying or deception, and nor is lying or deception allowed, let alone encouraged or promoted, in Islam. Taqiyah is, in extreme situations, and for the purposes of self-preservation, the concealing of one's beliefs, beliefs that deep down you still hold and haven't abandoned but have been forced to conceal against your will – and, on this basis, it is not only an Islamic principle or concept, but, let's be honest, it's common sense.

Question 28: What is "muta"? How can you justify such temporary marriages?

28.1 What is Muta?

Muta, or temporary marrage, is a controversial subject in any community and, some might say, rightly so. This publication does not promote muta; muta is something which is permissible in Islam; again, only under certain, specific, strict and extreme circumstances.

Permanent marriage, not temporary marriage, is the norm in Shia Islam, recommended and encouraged in the Holy Qur'an and in the traditions of the Prophet (SAW) and his Ahlul Bayt.

Temporary marriage is the exception to the rule and is supposed to be used as a last resort whenever permanent marriage cannot be afforded or things become extremely difficult to bear (for one who cannot get married). In certain circumstances it is allowed and avoids commiting adultery, which is a major sin.

What is ironic is that while disagreeing on the matter of temporary marriage, the scholars of some other Islamic schools of thought agree that if a man intends to marry a lady for a short period of time without telling her that he will be divorcing her after a period of time and hides his intentions then the marriage is still valid. In such a case, temporary marriage might, to some, seem more logical and just since the couple can actually agree on the terms and conditions beforehand with full honesty and transparency.

28.2 Evidence from the Holy Qur'an

"And all married women (are forbidden unto you) save those (captives) whom your right hands possess. It is a decree of Allah for you. Lawful unto you are all beyond those mentioned, so that ye seek them with your wealth in honest wedlock, not debauchery. And those of whom ye seek content (by marrying them), give unto them their portions as a duty. And there is no sin for you in what ye do by mutual agreement after the duty (hath been done). Lo! Allah is ever Knower, Wise." Ch.4: V: 24 [Surah Nisa]

Al-Tabari, in his Tafsir, says this verse and the reference to "mutual agreement" is a reference to muta.

The only real debate is whether the Holy Prophet (SAW) abolished it during his lifetime or whether it was Umar, the second caliph, who abolished it much later on? Some Ahle Sunnah scholars say Umar only reinforced what the Prophet had done. But the fact is that temporary marriage existed during the time of the Prophet and, at the very minimum, it was allowed by the Prophet for a time.

The key point about muta is not its theological basis, because it is exception to the rule, rather than the rule, but the fact that so few Shias actually engage in it.

Sadly, muta is used as a battering ram, as something to attack the Shias with, yet it is no less unappealing, no less odd, than the idea of four wives, which is also an exception to the rule, an exception to the norm, which is one wife.

Question 29: Why do Shias pay khums in addition to zakat?

29.1 Evidence from the Holy Qur'an

Khums is one of the pillars of Islam which was ordained by Allah (SWT) and practiced during the life of the Prophet (SAW). Khums means "one-fifth" and indicates that one-fifth of a person's excess income has to be dedicated, according to the Holy Qur'an, for the following: "And know that whatever profit you make, verily, one-fifth of it is assigned to Allah and to the Messenger and to his family and also the orphans, the destitute, and the wayfarer, if you have believed in Allah, and in that which We sent down to our servant Muhammad." Ch.8: V: 41 [Surah Anfaal].

Khums, in brief, means paying one-fifth of the surplus of one's income, after taking away the expenses of the person and his dependants. It consists of two equal parts: one being the share of the Imam, meaning that this part goes towards constructing mosques, Islamic seminaries, Islamic schools, libraries, hospitals or clinics, orphanages, the printing of the Holy Qur'an, hadith books, Islamic books and lectures and others things which might benefit, defend, or propagate Islam. The second part is the portion for the poor sayyids (descendants of the Prophet), since they are banned from receiving zakat (charity).

29.2 References from books of Ahle Sunnah

Many historical references from different schools of thought mention that khums existed during the time of the Prophet (SAW) and was banned during the time of the first and second caliphs – see reference books like the Sunan of Bayhaqi, the Musnad of Imam Ahmed ibn Hanbal and the

Tafsir of Tabari.

The interpretation by the Ahlul Bayt of the word "ghanimtum" in the Holy Qur'an, Ch.8: V 41 is "Everything you gained" - whether from war, work, trade, or other sources, since history testifies that the Prophet (SAW) took out one-fifth from the war booty, and also from assets other than the war booty during peacetime. Again, see, among other books, the Musnad of Imam Ahmed ibn Hanbal, one of the leading Sunni scholars of fiqh.

The importance given by the Prophet (SAW) to the issue of khums can also be seen in his advice to the delegation of Bani Abdul Qays. It seems that Bani Abdul Qays (which was a branch of Rabiah) was not a very strong tribe.

In order to travel to Madinah, they had to cross an area inhabited by the Muzar tribe, which was opposed to Islam and the Muslims. Consequently, the Bani Abdul Qays could not travel safely to Madinah except during the months in which warfare was forbidden, according to the Arab custom.

Here's the relevant hadith from Sahih al-Bukhari: Volume 1, Book 10, No. 501: Ibn Abbas narrates: "The delegates of the tribe of Abdul Qays came and said: `O Allah's Apostle! We are from the tribe of Rabia and between us and you stand the infidels of the tribe of Mudar, so we cannot come to you except in the Haram Months. So please order us some instructions that we may apply it to ourselves and also invite our people left behind us to observe as well. 'The Prophet (SAW) said: "I order you to believe in Allah, that is, to testify that none has the right to be worshipped but Allah (the Prophet pointed with his hand); to offer prayers perfectly, to pay Zakat, to fast the month of Ramadhan, and to pay the Khums."

Question 30: What is this "taqlid"? Why do Shias follow "marjas" and "mujtahids"?

30.1 What is taqlid ?

Taqlid literally means "to follow (someone)", "to imitate". In Islamic legal terminology it means to follow a "marja at-taqlid", literally a "source of emulation", a source of imitation, when it comes to religious laws and rulings. A marja is the senior-most mujtahid and a mujtahid is a person who is an expert on Islamic jurisprudence (fiqh); he is also called a faqih.

The orthodox Shia position is that a person should either be a mujtahid or a muqallid – a follower of a mujtahid.

It should be noted that taqlid pertains only to the realm of the shariah and the furu ud-deen; there can be no taqlid whatsoever in the matters of core belief (or usul ud-deen). The Holy Qur'an condemns such un-Islamic types of taqlid.

30.2 Evidence from the Holy Qur'an

The Holy Qur'an says in Surah Al Anbiya in relation to taqlid and ijtihad and mujtahids: "Question the people of remembrance if you do not know." (Ch.21:V7)

It also says, very clearly in Surah Tawba: "But why should not a party from every section of them (the believers) go forth to become learned in the religion, and to warn their people when they return to them, that they may beware?" (Ch. 9:V124).

This is about creating groups of scholars, aalims; not priests or clerics. Mujtahids are not priests – there are no Catholic-style priests or priesthood in Islam – they are scholars, engaged in much-needed ijtihad (literally: intellectual struggle). In Shia Islam, the gate to ijtihad is not closed – whereas in the Ahle Sunnah, the gate to ijtihad was largely closed a thousand or so years ago, with the formalisation of the four schools of fiqh, Hanafi, Shafi'i, Maliki and Hanbali.

30.3 Common sense

One of the problems plaguing modern Sunni Islam, which many Sunni intellectuals have identified, is the crisis of intellectual and theological leadership. Among the Ahle Sunnah, it is now possible for any person to issue a fatwa on this or that aspect of Islamic law or morality. Self-proclaimed shaykhs have proliferated! This problem does not exist in Shia Islam, where the ulema have to have studied for decades and won the respect of their peers before they can start issuing fatwas.

We seek expert guidance in every aspect of our lives – from accountants when we're doing our taxes, to doctors when we have health problems, to dentists when we have toothache, to engineers when we want to build something, to economists and financiers and stockbrokers when we want to make money - and yet when it comes to religion, our faith, our holy texts, the most important thing in our life, then we're told we should say, "No, I don't need any expert guidance, I'll work it out for myself".

If you've read and understood all the 6,000-odd verses of the Holy Qur'an, if you've read and understand all of the hundreds of Muslim and non-Muslim, Shia and Sunni, commentaries on the Holy Qur'an; if you've been through the hundreds and thousands of books of tradition, and the hundreds of thousands of ahadith from the Prophet, from the 12 Imams, from their companions and followers and students; if you've studied the biographies and the backgrounds of all the narrators of ahadith to work out who is reliable and who is unreliable; if you've studied, in full and in depth, Islamic law, theology, philosophy, history, ethics, then fine, go for it, do everything on your own, decide everything on your own. But if not, then why not take advantage of the fact, the blessing, that there is a group of people who have done all of those things and are offering us their services and their wisdom and their knowledge in the form of taqlid.

CHAPTER 4
THE HOLY QUR'AN AND
PRAYERS (SALAH)

Question 31: Do the Shias have another, different Holy Qur'an? Do you believe the Holy Qur'an is incomplete?

The answer to both the above is a definitive "No"! But this is a question that Shias have been asked for centuries, despite the fact that Shias use, and believe in, the same Holy Qur'an as the Ahle Sunnah. Whether you are Shia or Sunni, there is only one Holy Qur'an and no other.

31.1 Evidence from the Holy Qur'an

The Ahle Sunnah believe that the Holy Qur'an was first compiled by Uthman ibn Affan, the third caliph. But the Shias believe that the Hoy Qur'an was gathered and compiled by the Holy Prophet Muhammad (SAW) during his lifetime. The proof is in the tradition of Ghadeer Khumm: "I leave you the book…" How can the Prophet (SAW) refer to a "book" if it was not yet in existence?

The Holy Qur'an is protected from change or human interference or tampering, as the following verse of the

Holy Qur'an itself confirms: "Certainly, we revealed the Reminder and certainly we shall preserve it." Ch. 15: V:9 [Surah Al Hijr].

This is a guarantee from Allah (SWT) that the book is preserved. Unlike any other holy book, one of the miracles of the Holy Qur'an is that there are no changes to it wherever you go in the world.

Now, unfortunately, there have been some Shia narrations suggesting "tahrif", (changes to the text of the verses) may have occurred, but they are not considered authentic by the Shia scholars (ulema) and should be disregarded and ignored.

In fact, as the sixth Shia Imam, Jafar as Sadiq (AS), declared in a hadith narrated in Usul al-Kafi: "Test the various reports by the Book of God; whatever agrees with it take it, whatever disagrees with it reject it."

31.2 Other Shia scholars' verdicts

The completeness of the Holy Qur'an is so indisputable among the Shias that the greatest Shia scholar of Hadith, the 10th century aalim, Shaykh Saduq, wrote: "Our belief is that the Holy Qur'an which Allah (SWT) revealed to His Prophet Muhammad (SAW) is (the same as) the one between the two covers (daffatayn). And it is the one which is in the hands of the people, and is not greater in extent than that. The number of surahs as generally accepted is one hundred and fourteen ...And he who asserts that we say that it is greater in extent than that, is a liar."

Sayyid al-Murtadha, another prominent and classical Shia scholar states: "... our certainty of the completeness of the Holy Qur'an is like our certainty of the existence of countries or major events that are self evident."

Ayatullah al-Udhma Abul-Qassim al-Khoei, one of the most influential Shia scholars of the 20th century, teacher to the great contemporary marja Ayatullah al-Udhma Sistani, writes in his Tafsir al-Bayan that to hold a belief in: "...tahrif (corruption of the Holy Qura'nic text in any form) is nothing more than a delusion and an imagination, maintained by those with weak reasoning."

31.3 References from books of Ahle Sunnah

It seems strange that the Ahle Sunnah attack the Shias for supposedly believing in tahrif, in changes to the Holy Qur'an, while ignoring the fact that their own books of ahadith include traditions (wrongly) suggesting that tahrif has occurred.

For example, according to Umar and Aisha, there were once verses in the Holy Qur'an that were called the "verse of stoning" and the "verse of suckling" that were subsequently lost from the Holy Qur'an after the death of the Prophet (SAW).

According to Sunan Ibn Majah, Book of Suckling, Hadith No. 2020, Aisha said: "When the verse of stoning and verse of suckling descended, they were written on a piece of paper and kept under my pillow. Following the demise of Prophet Muhammad (SAW) a goat ate the piece of paper whilst we were mourning." A goat?

Hafiz Jalalludin as Suyuti narrates a similar tradition from Umar ibn Khattab, the second caliph, saying the verse of stoning was lost after the death of the Prophet (SAW).

Then there are the Sunni traditions suggesting the Holy Qur'an was once longer than it now is. For example, Suyuti narrates from Aisha, in his book, al-Durr al-Mansur: "Aisha narrated that during the lifetime of the Holy Prophet 200 verses were recited in Surah Ahzab but when Uthman collected the [text of the Holy Qur'an], he only succeeded in locating the present number of verses (which is 78)."

So where do the Sunni ulema believe the other 122 verses went? Such traditions, of course, are nonsense. The Holy Qur'an is the same Qur'an that the Prophet (SAW) left behind, and that Allah (SWT) says He will protect and preserve; any traditions which suggest otherwise – be they Shia or Sunni – should be rejected as false, as per the afore-mentioned hadith of Imam Jafar as-Sadiq (AS).

Question 32 : Why don't Shias wash their feet in wudhu, as the Ahle Sunnah do?

Shias wipe their feet in the wudhu while the Ahle Sunnah tend to wash their feet.

32.1 Evidence from the Holy Qur'an

According to Shias, the Qur'anic mandate for wudhu comes in the sixth verse of Chapter 5, Surah Maidah. The English translation by Abdullah Yusuf Ali – a famous Ahle Sunnah scholar and translator states: "O ye who believe! when ye prepare for prayer, wash your faces, and your hands (and arms) to the elbows; Rub your heads (with water); and your feet to the ankles. If ye are in a state of ceremonial impurity, bathe your whole body. But if ye are ill, or on a journey, or one of you cometh from offices of nature, or ye have been in contact with women, and ye find no water, then take for yourselves clean sand or earth, and rub therewith your faces and hands, Allah doth not wish to place you in a difficulty, but to make you clean, and to complete his favour to you, that ye may be grateful." Ch 5: V:16 [Suarh Maidah]

Those who practice the washing of their feet during wudhu argue that "your feet" in the Holy Qur'an is linked to washing the face, whereas the followers of the Ahlul Bayt argue that "your feet" is linked to rubbing the head; therefore, it should be wiped or rubbed, rather than washed.

Allah (SWT) did not repeat the verb for "feet", and joined "heads" and "feet" together under one verb "rub". This is exactly what he did for "faces" and "hands" that came under one verb "wash".

32.2 References from books of Ahle Sunnah

In support of the latter view, Abdullah ibn Abbas narrates from the Prophet (SAW), in a hadith included in the book of al-Shahrastani, a famous Ahle Sunnah scholar and philosopher of the 12th century, that, the companions used to rub their feet during the time of the Holy Prophet (SAW).

The fact is that all of the Muslims during the time of the Prophet (SAW) would have performed the wudhu in the same way. No disagreements would have occurred between them then since the Messenger of Allah was present among them to clarify the correct procedure.

The same situation existed during the time of the first caliph, Abu Bakr and no disagreements over the performance of wudhu have been reported from that time period either. This was also the case during the period of the second caliph, Umar ibn Khattab except for the fact, that he allowed wiping of the socks rather than the bare feet as the Holy Qur'an directs.

However, the disagreement regarding the performance of the wudhu began during the time of the third caliph, Uthman ibn Affan, after he began to wash his feet instead of wiping them.

The Sunni scholar Muttaqi al-Hindi, in his book Kanz al-Ummal mentions how the third caliph was the first to differ in performing the wudhu. According to Allama Muttaqi al-Hindi, more than twenty narrations - all narrated by the third caliph - are about his new manner of performing wudhu. These traditions indicate his responsibility for establishing the new method of washing, rather than wiping.

Now, some Muslims might argue that the washing of the feet leads to better cleanliness and hygiene than merely wiping the feet. However, Allah (SWT) is more aware of the advantages and disadvantages of washing versus wiping. It has been narrated that Imam Ali ibn Abu Talib (AS) once said, "If religion was according to human opinion, the bottom of the foot would be more worthy of wiping than the top. But I saw the Messenger of Allah (SAW) wiping the top of his feet."

32.3 Common sense

It is irrational, and incredible, that the same Ahle Sunnah scholars who say you must wash your feet, and not wipe your bare feet, also say that it is permissible to do wudhu by wiping wet hands over your socks or even over your shoes. How does this make sense? How is this consistent or logical?

Question 33: Why do Shias combine their prayers into three sittings?

The Shias allow for the combination of the 5 daily prayers (salah) into three times - whereas the majority of Ahle Sunnah scholars say that this is only permissible during journeys or in state of danger or war. Some Hanafi scholars don't accept the combination of prayers even in the afore-mentioned situations.

33.1 References from books of Ahle Sunnah

The combining of the prayer is based on the sunnah of the Holy Prophet (SAW), as narrated in leading Sunni books of hadith.

Sahih Muslim, Book 4, Hadith Number 1523: "Abdullah ibn Shaqiq reported: Ibn Abbas one day addressed us in the afternoon (after the afternoon prayer) till the sun disappeared and the stars appeared, and the people began to say: Prayer, prayer. A person from Banu Tamim came there. He neither slackened nor turned away, but (continued crying): Prayer, prayer. Ibn Abbas said: May you be deprived of your mother, do you teach me Sunnah? And then he said: "I saw the Messenger of Allah (SAW) combining the noon and afternoon prayers and the sunset and Isha prayers."

Sahih Muslim Book 4, Hadith Number 1520: "Ibn Abbas reported that the Messenger of Allah (SW) combined the noon prayer with the afternoon prayer and the sunset prayer with the Isha prayer in Madinah without being in a state of danger or rainfall." And in the hadith transmitted by Waki the words are: "I said to Ibn Abbas: What prompted him to do that? He said: So that his ummah should not be put to (unnecessary) hardship."

These ahadith appear in a chapter called, appropriately: "Permissibility of combining two prayers on a journey".

Others include this one from Sahih Muslim, Book 4, Hadith Number 1515: "Ibn Abbas reported: The Messenger of Allah (SAW) observed the noon and afternoon prayers together, and the sunset and Isha prayers together without being in a state of fear or in a state of journey."

33.2 Evidence from the Holy Qur'an

All Muslims observe the five daily prayers, but Shias believe these five prayers can be prayed at three (rather than five) different times - as stated in the Holy Qur'an: "Establish regular prayers at the sun's decline till the darkness of the night, and the recital of the Qur'an in the morning prayer; for the recital of the dawn is most witnessed." Ch.17:V 78 [Surah Bani-Israel]

How many prayer times are mentioned in this verse? Yes, three, not five: "Sun's Decline, Darkness of the Night, and the Morning Prayer."

Question 34: Why do Shias include "Aliyun Waliyullah" in the kalima and adhan?

34.1 Not compulsory (wajib)

The first point to remember is that this line of the adhan is not wajib. It is not considered to be a compulsory part of the adhan, iqamah or kalima and most Shia scholars state that it should not be recited with the niyyat (intention) of it being wajib. Most of them believe that it is something which is only mustahab, (recommended).

For example, the world's leading Shia aalim, Ayatullah al-Udhma Sistani says on his website, www.sistani.org: "Ash hadu anna Amiral Mo'mineena Aliyyan Waliyyullah (I testify that the Commander of the Faithful, Imam Ali (AS) is the vicegerent of Allah (SWT))" is not a part of either adhan or iqamah. But it is preferable that it is pronounced after "Ash hadu anna Muhammadan Rasulullah (SAW)" with the niyyat of Qurbat (nearness to Allah)."

34.2 References from books of Ahle Sunnah

However, the vast majority of scholars view the proclamation as a non-essential, non-mandatory, non-wajib, yet recommended part of the adhan. The logic is, among other things, that we have many narrations instructing us to proclaim the divine appointment of Imam Ali (AS) every time we proclaim the oneness of God and the prophethood of the Messenger.

The Sunni scholars Allama Tabari in his Tafsir and Shaykh Suleman ibn Ibrahim al-Hanafi al-Qandozi in his Yanabi al-Mawaddah both narrate that Abu Hurayrah, of all people, says that the Holy Prophet (SAW) told him: "It is written on the Divine Arsh [throne] that 'There is no god but Allah, the One Who has no associate; and Muhammad is my servant and Prophet, whom I helped through Ali ibn Abu Talib.'"

Hafiz Jalalladin as Suyuti, in his al-Durr al-Mansur, narrates how Anas ibn Malik said the Prophet told him that he had seen, on the Me'raj, written on the Arsh: "There is no god but Allah; Muhammad is the Prophet of Allah; I have given him support through Ali."

Hence according to Ahle Sunnah scholars, the coupling together of Muhammad (SAW) and Ali's (AS) names has not been done by Shia Muslims but by Allah (SWT) Himself in the highest of the Heavens!

34.3 Prophet's lifetime

Did this line appear during the lifetime of the Prophet? That of course is the crucial, historical question, and it has been narrated that it did.

The author of Kitab al-Salafa fi Amr al-Khilafa, Shaykh Abdullah al-Maraghi al-Misri, a leading Ahle Sunnah scholar, says that during the time of the Prophet (SAW), Salman al-Farsi attested to the imamat and wilayat of Ali ibn Abu Talib (AS) in the adhan and iqamah, straight after attesting to the prophethood of Muhammad (SAW). He did so after the coronation of Imam Ali (AS) by the Prophet (SAW) at Ghadeer Khumm.

In his book, Shaykh Abdullah narrates how a man came to see the Messenger of Allah (SAW) and said: "O Prophet of God, I have heard a thing which I have not heard before."

He [the Prophet] said: "And what is this?" The man replied: "After the shahadah to the risalah, Salman bore witness in his adhan a shahadah to the wilayah of Ali." The Prophet said: "You have heard a good thing."

34.4 Umar's innovation

Shias are attacked for supposedly adding a man-made line to the adhan and iqamah, relating to Ali ibn Abu Talib (AS). Yet the Ahle Sunnah ulema gloss over the fact that Umar ibn Khattab confessed to adding his own line, his own innovation to the adhan and iqamah.

The Sunni scholar, Imam Malik ibn Anas, reports in his Muwatta: "Yahya related to me from Malik that he had heard that the muadhin came to Umar ibn Khattab to call him to the morning (fajr) prayer and found him sleeping, so he said, "Prayer is better than sleep," and Umar ordered him to put that in the adhan for morning prayer (fajr)."

So let's be clear: the Ahle Sunnah are willing to say this line at fajr time, which was added to the adhan by Umar ibn Khattab but are unwilling to say a line about Ali (AS) which is written on the arsh of Allah (SWT) and which was approved by His Messenger? Does this make any sense?

Question 35: Why don't Shias cross their arms during the prayers?

Is it not sad and depressing that the Muslims cannot even agree whether the Prophet crossed his arms or not in prayers? The Holy Prophet (SAW) prayed at least 40,000 compulsory (wajib) prayers in front of his sahabah over the 22 years of his prophethood, yet Muslims cannot agree what he did with his hands while he was praying.

35.1 Ahle Sunnah internal divisions

It is important to note that the issue of arms is is not just a Shia-Sunni conflict; it is an intra-Ahle Sunnah conflict too. The Malikis, one of the four Ahle Sunnah schools of fiqh agree with the Shias in rejecting what they call "qabd" (or "grasping" - holding the left hand with the right), and opting for "sadl" (letting your hands drop at your side).

35.2 References from books of Ahle Sunnah

Allama Ibn Rushd, the famous 12th century Sunni scholar of Muslim Spain, writes in his famous legal manual, Bidayat al-Mujtahid: "The reason behind their differing is that there are some ahadith narrating the way the Prophet prayed which did not mention him placing his right hand over his left, and on the other hand, it was reported that the people were ordered to do that."

As for the traditions that Ibn Rushd is referring to, one of the most commonly cited is the hadith of Abu Humaid al-Sa'idi, narrated by Imam Ahmed ibn Hanbal, Abu Dawud and Bukhari, Volume 1, Book 12, Hadith Number 791:

"Narrated by Muhammad ibn 'Amr ibn 'Ata': "I was

sitting with some of the companions of Allah's Apostle and we were discussing about the way of praying of the Prophet. Abu Humaid as-Saidi said, "I remember the prayer of Allah's Apostle better than any one of you. I saw him raising both his hands up to the level of the shoulders on saying the Takbir; and on bowing he placed his hands on both knees and bent his back straight, then he stood up straight from bowing till all the vertebrate took their normal positions."

The statement "he stood up straight from bowing till all the vertebrate took their normal positions" is considered to be proof that the Holy Prophet (SAW) did not place his right hand over his left, for this is not the natural position at which the bones and limbs rest, rather, this is what is known as sadl - hands and arms at your side! If the Prophet placed his right hand over his left in the prayer, then (at least) one of the sahabah present would have objected to Abu Humaid's failure to report that in his narration. But none of them did so!

In another tradition, the Sunni scholar Allama Ibn Hajr Asqalani writes that "...when the Prophet would stand for salat, he would raise both hands to his ears, and after saying Takbeer would then drop his hands."

Drop, not cross, his hands! Sunni scholar Allama Ibn Abd al-Barr, in his book al-Tamheed, narrates: "Abdullah ibn al-Izar said, 'I used to make tawaf around the Kabah with Said ibn al-Jubayr [a leading member of the second generation of companions, the Tabi'een]. Once, Said saw a man placing one hand over the other, so he went to him, separated his hands, and then returned to me.'"

So, to sum up, the Shia practice of leaving one's arms at

one's side matches those of the sahabah and the children of the sahabah from the period straight after the Holy Prophet.

One final and important point to remember: not only do the Maliki Sunnis agree with the Shias on the uncrossing of the arms but even amongst the Hanafis, Hanbalis and Shafi'is there is no consensus on where exactly on the abdomen one's hands should be held, or how exactly both men and women should hold their hands during the salah (prayer).

Question 36: Why do Shias pray on a stone, on a piece of earth (a "sajdagaar" or "turbah")?

Prostrating on the earth (turbah) or nature made material does not in any way imply worshipping the earth or stone which one is prostrating upon. You are prostrating to Allah (SWT) and Him alone but remember: the prostration itself is a gesture of humiliation and insignificance before the Creator and if it is done on the dirt, on earth, then it will have more of an effect than prostrating on a man-made carpet. This is the philosophy behind the turbah, the sajdagaar.

36.1 Prophet's Sunnah

It is important to note that as with the uncrossing of the arms during the daily prayers, the use of a turbah is a practice associated with salah which has a firm foundation in the tradition, in the sunnah, of the Holy Prophet (SAW).

The Shias, after all, never forget that they are followers of the Prophet's Sunnah.

36.2 References from books of Ahle Sunnah

So how did the Prophet prostrate? According to Sahih Bukhari, Vol 1, Book 8, Number 378: "Maimuna (a wife of the Prophet) narrated, "Allah's Apostle used to pray on a 'khumra'."

The "khumra" is a small, palm-leaf mat, only big enough to place your face on during the sajdah.

Then there is Sahih Bukhari, Vol 1, Book 12, Number 798: "Abu Said al-Khudri says: "I saw Allah's Apostle prostrating in mud and water and saw the mark of mud on his forehead."

There are numerous such ahadith in Sahih Bukhari, the pre-eminent book of traditions for the Ahle Sunnah.

Al-Bayhaqi, Ahle Sunnah scholar of ahadith, in his Sunan, goes even further than Bukhari; he says the famous companion of the Prophet, Anas ibn Malik once narrated: "We used to pray with the Messenger of Allah during the enormous heat, and one of us would take pebbles in our hands and once they were cool, put them down and prostrate on them."

On pebbles!

36.3 Kerbala turbah

Now, of course, the majority of Shias pray on a "stone" which, on inspection, turns out to be baked piece of soil from the desert of Kerbala, in Iraq. It is not considered compulsory or wajib to pray only on the soil of Kerbala but Shia Muslims prefer to use such turbahs because the soil of Kerbala is the holiest of all soils. It is the soil that the Holy Prophet (SAW) held in his hand as he wept and prophesied the death of his youngest grandson. It is the soil under which the third holy Imam Husayn (AS) is buried; it is the soil that represents the very principles of Islam. So what better soil to worship on and prostrate on than the soil of Kerbala?

It is worth noting here: Shias are sometime smeared by some members of the Ahle Sunnah as "stone worshippers" for praying on a turbah. Yet, according to this logic, should Sunni Muslims then be referred to as "carpet worshippers" for prostrating on prayer rugs?

Question 37: Why do Shias say "Allahu Akbar" three times at the end of the prayer?

This issue is another point of contention between the Shi'a and the Ahle Sunnah. According to the Sunnah of Prophet that has reached us through Imams of Ahlul Bayt, a Muslim should commence the salah by loudly reciting "takbeer" (Allahu Akbar') and finish it by admitting the greatness and supremacy of Allah (SWT), by reciting "takbeer" thrice after the "tashahud" (the final kneeling prayer of the salah).

37.1 References from books of Ahle Sunnah

During the days of the Holy Prophet (SAW), the daily prayers were ended with the recitation of takbeer, and not with the turning of head from side to side.

In Sahih Bukhari Volume 1, Book 12, Hadith Number 803 states: "Abdulla ibn Abbas narrated: 'I used to recognize the completion of the prayer of the Prophet by hearing takbeer.'"

Similarly, it is stated in Sahih Muslim, Book 4, Hadith Number 1209: "Abdulla ibn Abbas said: 'We used to know that Allah's Messenger had finished his prayer when we heard the takbeer (Allahu Akbar).'"

In Ahle Sunnah tradition, the imam of the prayers turns right and left and prays the "salam" in a loud voice so it can be heard by those in the back rows. In Shia tradition, the imam of the prayers recites the salam in tashhahud and then loudly recites takbeer thrice and the congregation understands that the salah has finished.

37.2 Why don't the Shia turn their heads from side to side while reciting the "salam"?

To support this Shia stance there is a tradition from the Sunan of Abu Dawud, one of the six authentic Sunni books of ahadith, in which Holy Prophet holds Abdullah ibn Masud's hands and teaches him the recitation of tashahud.

In Sunan Abu Dawud, in the Chapter of Prayer (Kitab al-Salat): Hadith Number 965 states:

"Abdullah ibn Mas'ud narrated: '...the Apostle of Allah (SAW) caught hold of his (Ibn Mas'ud's) hand and taught him the tashahud during prayer.'"

He then narrated the tradition of tashahhud. This version adds: "When you say this or finish this, then you have completed your prayer. If you want to stand up, then stand, and if you want to remain sitting, then remain sitting."

There is no mention of the turning of the head!

Question 38: Why don't Shias offer "tarawih" prayers in the month of Ramadhan?

Shias, do not pray "tarawih", which refers to the extra congregational prayers performed by a number of Sunni Muslims at night in the holy month of Ramadhan.

Why not? Because Shias believe that there is no reliable, historical evidence that the Holy Prophet (SAW) ever performed such prayers.

The truth is that it is "bid'at", an "innovation", the word that the more extreme Wahhabi members of the Ahle Sunnah often use to smear the Shias. This is the opinion not of the Shia ulema but of Umar ibn Khattab, the second caliph of the Ahle Sunnah, who proudly introduced this particular bid'at of tarawih prayers.

Sahih Bukhari, vol 3, book 32, hadith number 227: Narrated Abu Hurayrah: ibn Shihab (a sub-narrator) said, "Allah's Apostle died and the people continued observing that (i.e. nawafil offered individually, not in congregation), and it remained as it was during the caliphate of Abu Bakr and in the early days of Umar's caliphate." Abdur Rahman ibn Abdul Qari said, "I went out in the company of Umar ibn Khattab one night in Ramadhan to the mosque and found the people praying in different groups. A man praying alone, or a man praying with a little group behind him.

So, Umar said, 'in my opinion it would better to collect these (people) under the leadership of one Qari (reciter) (i.e. let them pray in congregation!)'. So, he made up his mind to congregate them behind Ubai ibn Ka'b. Then on another night I went again in his company and the people were praying behind their reciter. On that, Umar remarked, 'what an excellent bid'at (i.e. innovation in religion) this is; but the prayer which they do not perform, but sleep at its time is better than the one they are offering.' He meant the prayer in the last part of the night, "the tahhajud".

The Shias prefer to pray Tahhajud, which Umar refers to here, at the end of this tradition, and which Umar admits is "better" than the tarawih that the Sunni Muslims recite in congregation during Ramadhan.

With due respect to our Ahle Sunnah brethren, Shias do not perform tarawih in Ramadhan. It is, like the line Umar added to the adhan for fajr, an innovation of the second caliph; it is not the sunnah of the Holy Prophet (SAW).

Question 39: How do Shias justify praying at graves?

39.1 Bid'at and Shirk

The Wahhabis and Salafis of the Ahle Sunnah are obsessed with graves. Praying at graves, they say, is banned and forbidden. Even touching the grave of the Holy Prophet (SAW) is considered to be prohibited. Consider how Shias are treated in Madinah, during Hajj and Umra, especially at Jannatul Baqi.

Ahle Sunnah rely on an alleged tradition of the Prophet: "May Allah's curse be upon the Jews and Christians for taking the graves of their Prophets as places of worship."

It is a nonsensical hadith. Jews and Christians have every right to respond to a Muslim who mentions this hadith: You hypocrites: you yourselves combine your Prophet's mosque with your Prophet's grave in Madinah!"

On a related note, if the Holy Prophet's grave is so unimportant, so unholy, if going to visit the Prophet in Madinah has no value, as some Wahhabis claim, then why did the first two caliphs of the Ahle Sunnah insist on being buried next to the Prophet's grave? And why did Aisha, the widow of the Prophet, refuse to allow the Prophet's eldest grandson Imam Hasan (AS) to be buried next to him?

Then there is the House of Allah (SWT), the Kabah, in Makkah, the holiest site in Islam, under which are buried the Prophet Ismail and his mother, Lady Hajira. Is it now shirk to visit the Kabah?

The Ahle Sunnah scholars have misunderstood the nature of prostrations, or sajdah, near graves – the issue is one of intention, niyyah. If the intention of the sajdah is to pray to the person buried in the grave, then this is of course forbidden and haram and an act of "shirk" (ascribing power to those other than Allah). But if the intention is to pray to Allah in the presence of a holy personality, then how is this wrong or shirk? Intention matters!

Remember: the Shias' prostrations during salah are always intended for Allah (SWT) and for Him alone. There are other prostrations which are unrelated to worship, and which are more symbolic and respectful but these are not forbidden either.

39.2 Evidence from the Holy Qur'an

The Holy Qur'an refers to prostrations which were carried out by or to our prophets, but which were not considered to be acts of shirk.

For example: "And when we told the angels, "prostrate yourselves before Adam!" - they all prostrated themselves, save Iblis, who refused and gloried in his arrogance: and thus he became one of those who deny the truth." Ch. 2: V:34 [Surah Al Baqarah].

And: "Behold! Joseph said to his father: "O my father! I did see eleven stars and the sun and the moon: I saw them prostrate themselves to me!" Ch. 12: V:4 [Surah Yusuf].

Were the angels committing shirk by prostrating themselves before Prophet Adam? Was Prophet Yusuf (Joseph) committing a sin by having this dream?

Question 40: What about intercession? Why do Shias pray to the Prophet and the Imams, and not to Allah?

40.1 What is intercession?

Intercession refers to the act of praying to Allah (SWT) on behalf of another - that is, the use of intermediaries to approach Allah (SWT), who pray to Him on our behalf by virtue of their higher status in the eyes of Allah (SWT).

The Sunni critics of intercession point to: "Thee (alone) we worship; Thee (alone) we ask for help." Ch 1:V5 [Surah Fateha].

However, intercession doesn't go against this verse of Surah Fateha; those of us who engage in intercession are still worshipping Allah (SWT) "alone" and asking only Allah (SWT) for help, but we are making this request through an intermediary. The prayer, ultimately, is still directed towards Allah (SWT), not towards the chosen inercessor or intermediary.

Common sense tells us that we ask others for help all the time in everyday life but we still recognize Allah (SWT) is sovereign over the entire universe. For example, when we are ill we go to doctors and take the medicine that they prescribe for us. Do Sunni critics of intercession like Wahhabis and Salafis practise what they preach? Do they deny themselves medicine and pray only to Allah (SWT) when they are ill? If not, why not? A doctor is, technically, an intercessor – the healing still, ultimately, comes from Allah (SWT).

To ask for help from someone else, whether medical or spiritual, is not an attack on the sovereignty of Allah (SWT); it is not an act of shirk.

40.2 Evidence from the Holy Qur'an

The Holy Qur'an addresses this issue in three manners. First, there are the verses which seem to negate intercession, such as: "O you who believe! spend out of what we have given you before the day comes in which there is no bargaining, neither any friendship nor intercession, and the unbelievers - they are the unjust." Ch.2: V254 [Surah Al Baqarah].

Then there are those verses that say that intercession is exclusively the domain of Allah (SWT), not humans - that is, that He and only He has the ability to intercede, such as: "Say: "To Allah belongs exclusively (the right to grant) intercession: to Him belongs the dominion of the heavens and the earth: In the End, it is to Him that ye shall be brought back." Ch.39:V44 [Surah Al Zumr].

Finally, there are those verses which contextualize and explain the first two categories and give the complete and final verdict about the validity and efficacy of intercession in Islam. They state that intercession is only the right of Allah (SWT), but He will, whenever He wishes, extend it to certain people in His creation.

So, for example: "...no intercessor can plead with Him except after His permission." Ch.10:V3 [Surah Yunus].

And Surah Maidah makes it even clearer: "O you who believe! Be careful of (your duty to) Allah (SWT) and seek means of nearness to Him, seek a means of approaching Him, and strive hard in His way that you may be successful." Ch.5:V35 [Surah Maidah].

This intermediary, this "wasilah", to use the terminology of the Holy Qur'an, can only be people like the Prophets and the Imams: "We sent not a messenger, but to be obeyed, in accordance with the will of Allah. If they had only, when they were unjust to themselves, come unto thee and asked Allah's forgiveness, and the Messenger had asked forgiveness for them, they would have found Allah indeed Oft-returning, Most Merciful." Ch.4:V64 [Surah Al Nisa].

Here is the best definition of intercession, or "tawassul" or "shifa'a", which justifies why the Shias go to see the Holy Prophet (SAW) in Madinah and try and pray near his grave: to ask the Prophet to ask Allah (SWT) for forgiveness, as mentioned in the Holy Qur'an, Ch4:V64. Shias are not praying to the Prophet or the Imams, but through them - to Allah (SWT)!

40.3 References from books of Ahle Sunnah

Tirmidhi, in his Sunan, relates, through his chain of narrators from Uthman ibn Hunayf, that a blind man came to the Holy Prophet (SAW) and said, "I've been afflicted in my eyesight, so please pray to Allah for me." The Prophet (SAW) said: "Go make ablution (wudhu), perform two rak'as of prayer, and then say: "Oh Allah, I ask You and turn to You through my Prophet Muhammad, the Prophet of mercy; O Muhammad (Ya Muhammad), I seek your intercession with my Lord for the return of my eyesight [and in another version: "for my need, that it may be fulfilled. O Allah, grant him intercession for me"]."

The Prophet (SAW) added, "And if there is some need, do the same."

In his discussion of the above sahih hadith, Shaykh Nuh Ha Mim Keller, the famous Sunni Sufi scholar and theologian, states: "The hadith explicitly proves the validity of supplicating Allah (SWT) (tawassul) through a living intermediary, as the Prophet (SAW) was alive at the time. The author of the article holds that the hadith implicitly shows the validity of supplicating Allah (tawassul) through a deceased intermediary as well, since the Prophet told the blind man to go perform ablution (wudhu) pray two rak'as, and then make the supplication containing the words, "O Muhammad, I seek your intercession with my Lord for the return of my eyesight," which is a call upon somebody physically absent, a state of which the living and the dead are alike.

Supplicating Allah (tawassul) through a living or deceased intermediary is, in the author's words, "not tawassul through a physical body, or through a life or death, but rather through the positive meaning attached to the person in both life and death, for the body is but the vehicle that carries that significance."

And perhaps the most telling reason, though the author does not mention it, is that everything the Prophet (SWT) ordered to be done during his lifetime was "legislation" "valid for all generations until the end of time unless proven otherwise by a subsequent indication from the Prophet himself. . ."

Shaykh Keller adds, in relation to the authencitiy of this important tradition: "This hadith was recorded by Bukhari in his "al-Tarikh al-Kabir", by Ibn Majah in his "Sunan", where he said it was rigorously authenticated (Sahih), by Nasa'i in "Amal al-yawm wa al-layla", by Abu Nu'aym in "Ma'rifa al-Sahaba", by Baihaqi in "Dala'il al-Nubuwwa", by Mundhiri in "al-Targhib wa al-Tahrib", by Haythami in "Majma' al-Zawa'id wa manba' al-Fawa'id", by Tabarani in "al-Mu'jam al-Kabir", by Ibn Khuzayma in his "Sahih", and by others. Nearly 15 hadith masters ("huffadh", hadith authorities with more than 100,000 hadiths and their chains of transmission by memory) have explicitly stated that this hadith is rigorously authenticated (sahih).

40.4 Common sense

As mentioned above, it has come with a chain of transmission meeting the standards of Bukhari and Muslim, so there is nothing left for a critic to attack or slanderer to disparage concerning the authenticity of the hadith. Consequently, as for the permissibility of supplicating Allah (tawassul) through either a living or dead person, it follows by human reason, scholarship, and sentiment, that there is flexibility in the matter. Whoever wants to can either take tawassul or leave it, without causing trouble or making accusations, since it has been this thoroughly checked ["Adilla Ahl al-Sunna wa al-Jama'a" , 79-83]."

CHAPTER 5
KERBALA AND MAJALIS

Question 41: Why do Shias wear black in Muharram?

Muharram is the first month of the Islamic calendar. It is the month in which Shia Muslims remember, commemorate and mourn the death of Imam Husayn (AS), the third Shia Imam and youngest grandson of the Holy Prophet (SAW).

41.1 Kerbala

Imam Husayn (AS) and 17 members of his family, including his six-month-old baby boy and another 92 companions (a total of 110) were killed in Kerbala, Iraq), on the 10th day of Muharram - or "Ashura" - in the year 680 AD, by the army of Yazid ibn Muawiya, the self-proclaimed caliph of the time.

It was a tragic and barbaric incident, involving one of the most important personalities in the history of Islam and the innocent young members of his family.

Now, all over the world the wearing of black clothes is recognised as a sign of mourning. In funerals, whether of Muslims or non–Muslims, people of different faiths and religions wear black as a sign of mourning. Yet when Shias wear black to commemorate the deaths of members of the

Prophet's household, his Ahlul Bayt, to grieve over Imam Husayn (AS), they are criticized. How is this fair?

41.2 References from books of Ahle Sunnah

Some members of the Ahle Sunnah claim that Shias look strange, odd, and fanatical for wearing black clothes in Muharram. One particularly provocative Sunni writer in Pakistan, Qadhi Mazhar Husayn, writes in his book: "Hum matam kyoon nahee kartey", claims that black clothes are the clothes of the people of hell and the clothes of "Firawn" (the Pharoah).

However, a number of other leading Ahle Sunah books confirm that the wearing of black is acceptable and a part of the sunnah. For example, the Sunni historian, Allama Tabari, in his "Tarikh", narrates from Aisha bint Abu Bakr that the Holy Prophet (SAW) himself, during his last days on earth, wore a black cloak.

The Tarikh Baghdad by Khateeb Baghdadi says that Jibraeel, the archangel, used to come to see the Prophet wearing a black cloak and a black turban.

And Tarikh Tabari says that Umar ibn Khattab, the second caliph of the Ahle Sunnah and considered by them to be one of the leading companions, was often sighted wearing black clothes – even on the hottest of summer days! Will they now compare Umar to the Pharoah? Or to the people of Hell?

It is worth bearing in mind that the Shias wear black clothes not just because black is the universal colour of sorrow and mourning, but because Lady Zainab (AS), the granddaughter of the Prophet (SAW), wore black to mourn for her brother Imam Husayn (AS).

Question 42: Why do Shias cry so much in Muharram?

Some Muslims claim that crying, and especially excessive crying, is wrong, uncalled-for and un-Islamic.

Yet crying is part and parcel of human nature and Islam. It was encouraged by the Holy Prophet (SAW) and in one famous hadith he states: "May you weep more and laugh less if you understand what is coming."

The Holy Qur'an has many verses which refer to the importance and validity of shedding tears: "And when they hear what has been revealed to the messenger you will see their eyes overflowing with tears on account of the truth that they recognize; they say: Our Lord! We believe, so write us down with the witnesses (of truth)." Ch. 5: V83 [Surah Maidah]

Then there is Surah Yusuf, and the reference to Yacub (Jacob), Ch.12:V84: "And he turned away from them, and said: O my sorrow for Joseph! And his eyes were filled (with tears) on account of the grief, then he repressed (grief).

In fact, the fourth Shia Imam, Zainul Abidin (AS), referred to this particular verse of the 12th surah when he was asked by a companion why he cried so much for his late father and brothers.

Shaykh Suleman ibn Ibrahim al-Hanafi al-Qandozi states in his book, Yanabi al-Mawaddah: "The grief of Imam Husayn (AS) is the grief on which not only humans, but even jinns, angels, animals, birds, the sky and trees, all lament and weep. It is written that the sky wept for forty days after the martyrdom of Imam Husayn (AS)."

Question 43: Why do Shias do "maatum" in Muharram?

"Maatum" is the symbolic beating of one's own chest or head as a physical sign of grief and sorrow.

The critics of the Shias claim it is an unIslamic and extremist practice, a symbol of the pre-Islamic period of "jahiliyyah" (ignorance) that was banned by the Holy Prophet (SAW).

But the truth is that maatum has Islamic origins and justifications.

43.1 Evidence from the Holy Qur'an

Turning again to the Holy Qur'an, we find in Ch.51:V29, in reference to Lady Sarah, wife of Prophet Ibrahim (Abraham), being told she was having a baby: "Then came forward his wife in grief, she hit her face and said (what! I) an old barren woman?" [Surah Dhariat].

43.2 References from books of Ahle Sunnah

There are many references to maatum-like behaviour during and after the time of the Prophet in the books of the Ahle Sunnah.

Ahle Sunnah scholars, for instance, narrate how Owais al-Qarni, a companion of the Holy Prophet (SAW) who was in Yemen during the battle of Ohud, broke his own teeth when he heard that the Prophet (SAW) had been hurt in battle and had lost some of his teeth. The Prophet (SAW) did not criticise or denounce Owais for doing so.

Then there is the aftermath of the Battle of Ohud, in which the Holy Prophet (SAW) established a period of mourning, including maatum, for his uncle Hamza who had been killed in the fighting. Shibli Numani narrates: "The Prophet ordered the folk of Madinah to go to Hamza's house and to cry and grieve over him."

Then there is the example of Aisha bint Abu Bakr; the classical Sunni scholar Allama ibn Kathir narrates from Aisha that when the Holy Prophet (SAW) passed away she said, "I got up beating my chest and slapping my face along with other women."

Allama Muttaqi al-Hindi, the Sunni scholar, narrates: "When Hazrat Umar heard of Nu'man ibn Muqrin's death he beat his head and screamed, "O what a pity that Nu'man died".

Umar could do maatum for Nu'man, who was one of his military commanders and died in battle, but when Shias do the same for Imam Husayn (AS), the beloved grandson of the Holy Prophet (SAW), it is frowned upon and termed as an innovation (or "bid'at"). Does this make any sense?

Question 44: Isn't the display of an "alam" prohibited and a form of shirk?

44.1 Religious symbols

"Alam" means a "flag", a "standard" or "sign" in Arabic. It is a symbol and, let us be clear, Shias do not worship these standards.

All religions, of course, have symbols. Without symbols or rituals there is no religion. Look at the world's leading religions – the Christians, Jews, Hindus – all are full of different religious symbols.

The alam is of spiritual significance for the Shia Muslims. Although all Shias, including those of Iraq, Iran, Afghanistan, Lebanon, Azerbaijan, Turkey, Bahrain, Saudi Arabia, and Syria carry some form of alam or another in their Ashura processions, remembering Imam Husayn (AS), those in the Indian subcontinent are of a different kind and are given a more deeper, spiritual significance.

Historically, the Prophet's family had a unique flag (alam) that specifically represented the Bani Hashim clan. One honorable member of the family would always be chosen to carry this on a journey or in battle. Originally, it was green in colour and given to the first Shia Imam, Ali ibn Abu Talib (AS), by the Prophet (SAW) himself. Imam Ali (AS) gave this alam to his sons Imam Hasan (AS) and then to Imam Husayn (AS) who passed it to His half-brother Abbas ibn Ali (AS), who held this alam till his last breath in the Battle of Kerbala.

Remember: every country and group has a symbol or flag, not just the Shias. The alam is simply a sign, a symbol, of the Prophet's holy household, his Ahlul Bayt.

Some people do not like the way the alams are made. But each community should be left to their own; nobody has the right to force these rituals on others or force others to abandon such rituals. They are part and parcel of an ever-evolving remembrance of the tragedy of Kerbala and Imam Husayn (AS). They are not compulsory or wajib. Unfortunately, some individuals get very defensive and get caught up in these new and petty divisions. It is important to understand the reason and history behind these rituals.

44.2 Evidence from the Holy Qur'an

Once again, we can refer to the Holy Qur'an to understand the values of symbols in Islam, and their power. In Surah Yusuf, the Prophet Yusuf (Joseph) said: "Go with this my shirt, and cast it over the face of my father: he will come to see (clearly). Then come ye (here) to me together with all your family." Ch. 12: V93 [Surah Yusuf].

Unfortunately, a number of Muslims from Ahle Sunnah schools – for instance, the Wahhabis of Saudi Arabia - treat symbols as if they are prohibited and haram and without any reference to the teachings of the Holy Qur'an or the Holy Prophet (SAW). This creates unnecessary misunderstanding and has damaging effects on Islamic culture and history. A number of very important and historic sites have been demolished in places like Makkah and Madinah because of the incorrect belief that symbols are prohibited and evidence of shirk.

Question 45: Weren't Shias responsible for killing Imam Husayn (AS)?

This is a very serious allegation made against Shia Muslims by some ill-informed or ill-intentioned individuals.

45.1 Invitation to Kufa

The claim is that it was Shias in Kufa who wrote letters to Imam Husayn (AS) inviting him to Kufa and it was they who then betrayed him. Imam Husayn (AS) had sent his cousin, Muslim ibn Aqeel to go and assess the situation in Kufa, where the people of Kufa promptly gave allegiance (bay'at) to him before turning against him once the army of Yazid arrived. The Kufans failed to join the army of Husayn (AS) or go out to protect him from his enemy and now, 14 centuries later, some Muslim and non-Muslim commentators claim that Shias do maatum out of "guilt" for having failed and betrayed their Imam, Husayn (AS), on the day of Ashura. This, however, is a historical nonsense which is designed to try and shift the blame away from those really responsible for the murder of Imam Husayn (AS) and his family in Kerbala.

45.2 Historical facts

Kufa, contrary to conventional wisdom, was not a "Shia city". According to the famous Sunni scholar and biographer, Shibli Numani, Kufa was a city in Iraq that had been founded by Umar ibn Khattab, during his caliphate, as a military fort for his soldiers and supporters.

Imam Ali (AS) then moved there during his caliphate, in order to keep an eye on the rebellious antics of Muawiya ibn Abu Sufyan in neighbouring Syria. After his death, according to Sunni historian Allama Tabari, the Shias of Kufa, who had accompanied Ali ibn Abu Talib (AS) to that city, were rounded up, tortured and killed by Ziyad, one of the appointees of Muawiya (and the father of Ubaidullah ibn Ziyad, who was governor of Kufa during the Kerbala tragedy).

Abdullah ibn Abbas, the respected companion and cousin of the Prophet, even warned Imam Husayn (AS) when he was leaving Madinah that the people of Kufa were "deceitful people" who could not be trusted.

Then there is the key historical fact that the army of Yazid which first starved and then killed Imam Husayn (AS) and his followers was from Syria, not Kufa. It is narrated by Shah Abdul Aziz, the Sunni scholar: "The Syrian forces upon orders of Yazid and the efforts of Chief of hatred and fitnah - Ibn Ziyad martyred Imam Husayn in Kerbala."

The history of Kerbala has been recorded in a number of Ahle Sunnah books, and it is very clear from this history who was and wasn't responsible for the killing of Imam Husayn (AS). Today, those Muslims who pretend Yazid ibn Muawiya was not responsible for it are like those neo-Nazis who deny that Hitler was responsible for the Holocaust.

Question 46: Isn't Ashura a day of fasting, not mourning?

Some members of the Ahle Sunnah sadly seem to want to devalue the theological and spiritual significance of Ashura and to distract Muslims from the historical events of Ashura. So they claim, for instance, that it is a day of fasting, not a day of mourning.

46.1 References from books of Ahle Sunnah

An (unreliable) tradition in the Sunni books claims that when the Holy Prophet (SAW) came to Madinah in 622 AD, he found the Jews of the city were fasting. He enquired what the fast was for and was told that it was a "blessed day": the day that Prophet Musa (Moses) had left Egypt. The Holy Prophet of Islam (SAW) apparently told the Jews that we are "closer to Musa than you", and then commanded Muslims to also fast on this day" – according to Sahih Bukhari.

It is also claimed, in the Musnad of Imam Ahmed ibn Hanbal, that the Prophet (SAW) said to his companions: "Observe fasting on the day of Ashura, but differ from the Jews and fast one day before it and one day after it."

The Shias do not believe that these traditions are authentic or worth following because:

- the authenticity of hadith is questionable: the three narrators of it are Muawiya ibn Sufayan, who became a Muslim just before Prophet's(SAW) death and wasn't present when the Prophet (SAW) arrived in Madinah (and, of course, was an opponent of the children of Ali ibn Abu Talib (AS)); Abu Hurayrah, who became a Muslim in 629 AD and, again, wasn't present in Madinah when the Prophet (SAW) arrived and allegedly witnessed the Jews fasting on Ashura (and whose testimony, as discussed earlier, is unreliable); and Abdullah ibn Abbas, who was a child in 622 AD and whose alleged testimony, therefore, can't be relied upon on this occasion.

- Ashura has more than one meaning. The old, pre-Kerbala meaning of Ashura is "the tenth", that is, the tenth of any month. Just because the Prophet (SAW) supposedly arrived in Madinah on "the tenth", it doesn't mean he arrived on the tenth of Muharram.

- The Jewish calendar is only semi-lunar and does not therefore permanently correlate to the fully lunar Islamic calendar so even if such a festival did exist in the Jewish calendar, it wouldn't correspond with the 10th of Muharram year after year.

46.2 Jewish fasts

However, above all else, the fundamental question the Shias ask, in response, is this: how do we know such a Jewish fast even existed? The evidence suggests that there is no such fast, as described by Bukhari, marking Prophet Musa's departure from Egypt.

The fact is that Jews fast on the following seven days of the year:

- The Fast of Yom Kippur
- The Fast of Tisha B'Av
- The Fast of Gedaliah
- The Fast of the 10th of Tevet
- The Fast of the 17th of Tammuz

- The Fast of Esther
- The Fast of the Firstborn

None of these fasts commemorate the day Prophet Musa left Egypt. The Bukhari hadith refers to a fictitious Jewish fast in order to try and ascribe another, non-Husayn-related meaning to Ashura.

One final point worth considering here: let's assume Bukhari and company are correct for a moment, and that there was a Prophet Musa-inspired Jewish day of fasting which coincided with the day of Ashura in Muharram. Even then, would such a Jewish day of fasting overshadow or trump the importance and significance of Imam Husayn's (AS) sacrifice and death in Kerbala on Ashura? How can that be possible?

Question 47: How can Shias trust the Kerbala story?

47.1 Background

A number of individuals assume that the story of Imam Husayn (AS) and the Kerbala tragedy is a collection of legends and folktales. On the contrary, the fact is that there are few events in Islamic history as documented and reliably-narrated as the event of Kerbala in 680 AD.

Reliable Muslim historians have reported the key episodes with trustworthy and verified chains of transmission from the 7th and 8th centuries, and their narrations corroborate one another.

Abu Mikhnaf, the Kufan historian, wrote the first "Maqtal al-Husayn" in 788 AD, that is, within 100 years of the event of Kerbala and much earlier than some of the histories that were written about other prophets and religious events. The Christian Gospels, for example, were compiled more than a hundred years after Jesus departed from this earth.

And compare for example Abu Mikhnaf's Maqtal - which became the source for later Muslim histories like Tabari and Baladhuri - with, say, Sahih Bukhari, which was compiled more than 200 years after the death of the Holy Prophet (SAW).

47.2 References from books of Ahle Sunnah

Classical Sunni historians like Tabari and Baladhuri authenticated and incorporated Abu Mikhnaf's work into their own. Volume 19 of the History of Tabari, the caliphate of Yazid ibn Muawiya, gives a very detailed account of Yazid's role in the Kerbala tragedy, as well as the battle in

Kerbala itself and the various deaths. This volume also includes eyewitness statements.

47.3 Other historians

Western historians have also covered the events in Kerbala: Edward Gibbon, the 18th century English historian, writes in his "Decline and fall of the Roman Empire": "In a distant age and climate the tragic scene of the death of Husayn will awaken the sympathy of even the coldest reader."

The famous 19th century Scottish historian Thomas Carlyle writes: "The best lesson which we get from the tragedy of Kerbala is that Husayn and his companions were rigid believers in God. They illustrated that the numerical superiority does not count when it comes to the truth and the falsehood. The victory of Husayn, despite his minority, marvels me."

There also exist a number of authentic histories by leading Shia scholars such as Shaykh Abbas Qummi and Shaykh al-Mufid.

All of these history books - Sunni and Shia, Muslim and non-Muslim - confirm that the tragedy of Kerbala happened in the year 680 AD, that Imam Husayn (AS) and his followers were killed in the desert after being starved of food and water, and that Yazid ibn Muawiya's army was responsible for this heinous crime.

Question 48: Wasn't Imam Husayn (AS) wrong to revolt against the ruler of his time, Yazid ibn Muawiya?

Some contemporary Sunni figures like India's Zakir Naik have claimed that the Kerbala tragedy was a "political war" based only on a "difference of opinion" between Yazid and Imam Husayn (AS).

Some medieval Sunni scholars, like Ibn Taymiyah, the ideological forefather of the Wahhabis, argue that Imam Husayn (AS) had "political aims" and he was a "rebel". This is as absurd as it is offensive.

48.1 Yazid was not the legitimate ruler

Muawiya, under the terms of the "peace treaty" with the second Imam, and fifth caliph, Imam Hasan (AS), had no right to make Yazid his successor, that is, the next caliph after him. According to the explicit terms of that treaty, the caliphate of the Muslims was supposed to revert back to Imam Hasan (AS) and, if Imam Hasan (AS) had passed away, to Imam Husayn (AS). So if Imam Husayn (AS) had indeed been revolting against Yazid ibn Muawiya he would have been perfectly within his rights to do so. Imam Husayn was the legitimate caliph; Yazid was a usurper.

48.2 Imam Husayn's mission

Remember: according to the Holy Prophet's (SAW) ahadith, narrated by Sunni and Shia ulema alike, Hasan and Husayn were "Imams, whether sitting or standing" and "chiefs of the youths of Paradise".

Imam Husayn's (AS) mission was not a military mission; he did not set out to fight Yazid or go to war with the Ummayad tribe. He said very explicitly before leaving Madinah: "I am setting out from here to reform the ummah (followers) of my grandfather". Imam Husayn (AS) never said he was after power or authority. He made it clear that he wanted reform; his mission was to restore Islamic practices within the Islamic community.

There is no record in any book of Imam Husayn (AS) ever, not even once, asking for power in any conversation with any member of Yazid's government or army. He also refused to take his main warriors with him to fight in Kerbala. His five best and bravest warriors were: Abbas, Muslim ibn Aqeel, Abdullah ibn Jafar, Muhammad Hanafiya and his own son, and the fourth Imam, Zain ul Abidin (AS). Muawiya used to say that these five warriors were sufficient to conquer the whole of Arabia – yet, on Ashura Day , only one of these five was available to Imam Husayn (AS) to fight - Abbas - and even he was forbidden from fighting. Does this sound like the behaviour of a military commander? A man bent on war and bloodshed?

And, never forget, Imam Husayn (AS) took women and children with him on his journey to Kufa, against advice of elders like Abdullah ibn Abbas.

He wanted to show the world that he was not embarking on a military mission or expedition.

As Charles Dickens, the famous novelist and scholar of the West, has noted: "If Husayn fought to quench his worldly desires, then I do not understand why his sisters, wives and children accompanied him. It stands to reason therefore that he sacrificed purely for Islam."

It is sad that even non Muslims like Dickens and Gibbon can readily acknowledge and accept what Imam Husayn (AS) did and what he achieved in Kerbala, while many Muslims continue to ignore or question his supreme sacrifice.

Question 49: Don't the Shias exaggerate how bad Yazid was?

Apologists for Yazid within the Ahle Sunnah claim that he should be exempted from criticism because he was part of the naval expedition that conquered Constaninople and that was praised and prophesied by the Messenger of Allah (SAW) himself.

This however, is a convenient and self-serving (Ummayad) myth.

49.1 References from books of Ahle Sunnah

There is a tradition from the Holy Prophet (SAW), narratd in Sahih Bukhari, that the members of the first army to invade "Caesar's city", Constantinople in modern-day Turkey, would go to Heaven. Yazid's defenders claim he was a member of this army and therefore is Heaven-bound.

However, according to the leading, classical Sunni historian and biographer, Allama ibn Hajar Asqalani, in his Fath al-Bari, says it is a weak if not worthless hadith (about "Caesar's city"). It has been narrated, he notes, only by Syrians, including Sawaar bint Yazeed, an openly anti-Ali (AS) individual who always tried to promote and praise Yazid ibn Muawiya.

The truth is that Yazid was too drunk to join the expedition to Constantinople.

In volume 3 of his Tarikh Kamil, the classical Sunni scholar Allama ibn Athir states that in 50 Hijri, Muawiya sent a huge army to Caesar's city (Constantinople) and appointed Sufyan ibn Au'f as commander of that army. He also ordered his son Yazid to join the army. Yazid made various excuses, including that he was feeling ill. Muawiya, writes ibn Athir, freed his son from the obligation of participating in the expedition. During the subsequent war with the Roman Empire, the Muslim army suffered from illness and a shortage of supplies. When Yazid heard of this calamity, he started singing: "I have no care for the soldiers' hardship in the place of Farookhdana, where they are suffering with fever and many calamities. Here I am enjoying with my wife…"

It is also recorded in Muruj al-Dhahab by the famous Sunni historian Allama Masudi: "Mu'awiya received information on the progress of the army and conveyed this news to Yazeed who said, "In this case I shall convene a function in home, joined by my fellow drinkers".

So it is clear from his own testimony, as included in Sunni history books, that Yazid was not part of the army which conquered Constantinople, and that the hadith which claims the members of that army were guaranteed Heaven is, according to Sunni scholars like ibn Hajar Asqalani, weak and unreliable to begin with.

49.2 Yazid's crimes

Whether or not Yazid conquered Constantinople is, frankly, irrelevant given the crimes and sins he openly committed later on in life, during his caliphate.

Some Wahhabis want to pretend there is a "difference of opinion" about Kerbala but what about the massacre in Madinah two years after the Kerbala incident, and what about the burning of the Kabah by Yazid's forces less than three years later?

In volume 19 of Tarikh Tabari, the famous Sunni historian Allama Tabari documents how Yazid carried out these outrageous and unforgivable abuses in Madinah and Makkah.

Allama ibn Athir, the Sunni scholar, has written how thousands of Muslims in Madinah were killed and beheaded, thousands were made slaves, and more than a thousand women raped, by Yazid's army. Allama ibn Qutaybah has described how babies in Madinah were snatched from their mothers' arms and thrown against the walls; horses from Yazid's army were allowed to graze and urinate inside Masjid al-Nabawi, the Prophet's (SAW) mosque in Madinah.

The sahabah, the companions, and their descendants, were murdered en masse by the Syrian army in this attack on Madinah – the historians note that not a single survivor of the Battle of Badr was left alive by Yazid's soldiers.

Then, the following year, as Tabari and others record, the army of Yazid moved onto Makkah and attacked the Kabah from the surrounding hilltops, using fireballs which set the cloth of the Kabah on fire!

Can you imagine the reaction in the Muslim world if the US or British or Israeli airforces bombed Makkah and Madinah and set the Kabah on fire? There would be outrage, anger, mass uprisings and anti-Western revenge attacks. Yet, a Muslim ruler, a so-called caliph, sets fire to the Kabah, rapes and loots the people of Madinah, and the Muslims are expected to forget this episode, and not hate or curse him?

Question 50: Imam Husayn (AS) lost the battle of Kerbala, didn't he?

This is based on the fact that Yazid survived and Imam Husayn (AS) was killed. So some, wrongly, claim that Yazid "won" and Imam Husayn (AS) "lost".

50.1 Imam Husayn's (AS) mission

However, this is a total and almost willful misunderstanding and under-estimation of what Imam Husayn's (AS) mission was. It was not a political challenge or a military revolt against the Ummayad regime; it was a mission for truth: the truth of Islam, of Allah's existence, of the Prophet's message the truth of Husayn's (AS) own imamat and wilayat.

All of Imam Husayn's (AS) statements and actions in the run-up to Kerbala show that he was well aware of the fact that a victory achieved through military strength and might is always temporary and short-lived, because another stronger power can, over the course of time, overturn it and bring it down. But a victory achieved through suffering, through sacrificing and struggling, is everlasting and leaves a permanent and unshakeable imprint on man's consciousness and emotions.

In Kerbala, as the Shia historian S.H.M Jafri observes in his book, "The Origins and Early Development of Shi'a Islam", the natural process of conflict and struggle between "action" and "reaction" was at work. The Prophet's Islamic teachings had succeeded in suppressing the jahilliyah (ignorance) and ultra-conservatism and backwardness of the desert Arabs. But, within fifty years of his death, this Arab jahilliyah had revitalised itself as a forceful reaction to challenge the Holy Prophet's teachings once again. The strength of this corrupt reaction, embodied in the corrupt and un- Islamic personality of Yazid, was powerful enough to suppress or at least deface the Prophet's original message. Thus, in the mind of Imam Husayn (AS), Islam was now in dire need of reactivation, of action, against the old Arab reaction and thus it required a complete shake-up and overhaul, a complete revolution.

Imam Husayn's (AS) mission was based on the realisation that simply by picking up weapons and fighting, simply by using violence and combat, he could not save Islamic action and consciousness. In his view, it needed a shaking of hearts and minds; it needed a jolt to the emotions. And this, the Imam decided, could only be achieved through pain and self-sacrifice, through martyrdom; through a physical and spiritual mission not seen before in human history and not seen again since.

Imam Husayn (AS) did not set out to fight and win a military battle against Yazid and his cronies so the fact that Husayn was killed, and all his companions were killed - by a far bigger, much more heavily-armed army - is irrelevant to the debate over victory versus defeat.

After all, you measure whether someone has won or lost in a battle, in a struggle, in a fight, based on what they said their aims were before the fight. The history of Kerbala shows Yazid failed to achieve his aim, even after killing Imam Husayn (AS). In contrast, Imam Husayn (AS) achieved his original aims of standing up for truth and reform and Islam, and not bowing his head to a tyrant.

50.2 Yazid's aim

Yazid's aim was very explicit – to get bay'at (allegiance) from Imam Husayn (AS), in order to stabalise his own (illegitimate) caliphate.

Imam Husayn's (AS) aim was not to bow his head to tyranny, to illegitimate rulers but to stay on the true path of Islam, of his grandfather, the Holy Prophet (SAW). He refused to be intimidated by the threat of death. "Death for me is a blessing," Imam Husayn (AS) famously remarked in front of the army of Yazid.

So who won? The side of Imam Husayn (AS), never bowed its head and never gave allegiance to either Yazid or his various cronies. Bay'at was not given! And history testifies that his son, the fourth Shia Imam, Zain ul Abidin (AS), never gave his allegiance to Yazid in the palaces of Kufa or Shaam (Syria), nor was he ever asked to give allegiance by Yazid.

In fact, after the Battle of Kerbala, no Shia Imam was ever again asked to give allegiance by any future Ummayad or Abbasid caliph. What does Imam Sajjad (AS) say to a man who abuses him in Damascus? He says: "Wait for the adhan, then see, who won and who lost…"

Today, thanks to Imam Husayn's (AS) sacrifice, the adhan still contains the name of Muhammad (SAW); Islam in its original form still exists.

50.3 The role of Lady Zainab and Lady Umm Kulthum

Had it not been for Lady Zainab (AS) and her sister Lady Umm Kulthum (AS), the two sisters of Imam Husayn (AS) and granddaughters of the Prophet (SAW), Muslims would not have known the objectives of the supreme sacrifice performed by Imam Husayn (AS). They completed his mission and spread the message of Kerbala.

We would not have understood his embodiment of the eternal struggle of good against evil, truth against falsehood, justice against injustice; his eternal symbolism for all revolutions of the oppressed against the oppressors.

Without them spreading the word in the weeks and months after the tragedy on Ashura, his aim would have been lost and the great tragedy of Kerbala would have - God forbid – been forgotten by history or buried under a mountain of Ummayad distortions and misinterpretations.

Muslims have to accept and acknowledge this important reality, to understand it and spread it far and wide. Only then can we do justice to the roles of both Imam Husayn (AS) and Lady Zainab (AS).

Due to Lady Zainab (AS), Imam Husayn (AS) is respected by all Muslims - both Sunnis and Shias - as the 'Prince of Martyrs'. Yazid is only remembered by all Muslims, for exactly what he was: a cruel, evil, tyrannical enemy of Islam.

The clearest sign of her own personal victory is that if you go to Damascus in Syria today, you will see the magnificent rawdha (shrine) of Lady Zainab (AS). The area near the shrine is known as Zainabiyya. The local Syrians praise and honour her; but there is no mention of Yazid, no memorial for Yazid!

So, to reiterate and conclude, the loser was Yazid. The true victors at Kerbala were Husayn (AS) and the original and authentic religion of Islam, of Prophet Muhammad (SAW).

References

Al-Durr al-Mansur by Jalaluddin al-Suyuti

Al-Muraja'at - The Right Path by Sayyid 'Abd al-Husayn Sharaf al-Din al-Musawi, translated by Yasin al-Jibouri

Al-Sawa'iq al-Muhriqah by Ibn Hajar al-Haythami al-Makki

A Shi'ite Encyclopedia edited by Ali Abbas [http://www.al-islam.org/encyclopedia]

Decline and fall of the Roman Empire by Edward Gibbon

Hadith Literature: It's Origin, Development, & Special Features by Muhammed Zubayr Siddiqui

Inquiries about Shi'a Islam by Sayyid Moustafa al-Qazwini

Origins and Early Development of Shi'a Islam by S.H.M. Jafri

Peshawar Nights by Sultanu'l-Wa'izin Shirazi, translated by Hamid Quinlan and Charles Ali Campbell

Sahih Bukhari by Imam Muhammed ibn Ismail Bukhari, translated by Mohammed Muhsin Khan

Sahih Muslim by Imam Muslim, translated by Abdul Hamid Siddiqui

Sirat-un-Nabi by Shibli Numani

Sunan al-Bayhaqi by Imam al- Bayhaqi

Tafisr al Kabir by Fakhruddin al-Razi

Tafsir al-Tabari, by Muhammad ibn Jarir al-Tabari

Tarikh al-Rusul wa al-Muluk or *Tarikh al-Tabari* by Muhammad ibn Jarir al-Tabari

Then I Was Guided by Sayyid Muhammad Tijani al-Samawi

The Succession to Muhammad by Wilferd Madelung

The Unique Necklace: Al-Iqd Al-Farid (The great books of Islamic civilization) by Ibn Abd Rabbih